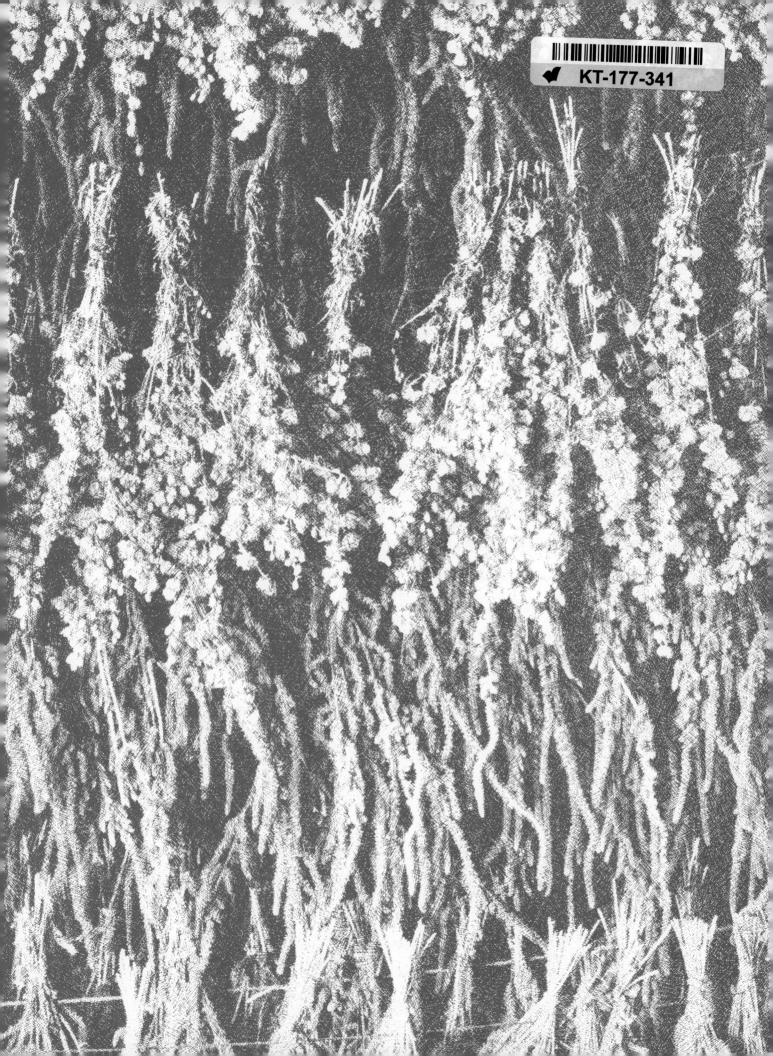

The Complete Book of
Dried Flowers

The National Trust

The Complete Book of
Dried Flowers

Malcolm Hillier & Colin Hilton

Published in association with
The National Trust

DORLING KINDERSLEY
LONDON

Remembering Juliet Glynn Smith
whose inspiration set us off on this journey

Art editor Sally Smallwood
Senior editor David Lamb

Editor Jane Laing
Designer Jane Warring

Editorial Director Jackie Douglas
Art Director Roger Bristow

Still-life photography by Andreas Einsiedel

First published in Great Britain in 1986 by
Dorling Kindersley Publishers Limited,
9 Henrietta Street, London WC2E 8PS
in association with The National Trust
Reprinted 1987

British Library Cataloguing in Publication Data
Hillier, Malcolm
   The complete book of dried flowers.
   1. Flowers – Drying
   I. Title   II. Hilton, Colin
   745.92   SB447
   ISBN 0-86318-177-5

Reproduced in Singapore
Printed and bound in Hong Kong

CONTENTS

Introduction

Flowers are an important part of our lives. They bloom wild in the countryside in wondrous array, and blossom in even the densest parts of our cities. There they are at all the important occasions in our lives, bringing great joy and happiness. Quite simply, they transform our spirits.

Why dried flowers?
Whilst there is a precious quality about the impermanence of fresh flowers (the fleeting life of a bowl of scent-laden sweet peas or a vase spilling over with great summery paeonies, for example), it is exciting to know that the pleasure flowers bring can have a permanence. The flowers, leaves and seedheads of nearly every plant can be dried and preserved.

When certain flowers and leaves are dried they retain their perfume and these in particular have been used since the earliest times both to adorn and to perfume rooms. Rose petals were scattered, sweet-scented rushes were strewn on floors and filigree containers and cloth bags were filled with perfumed leaves and flowers to sweeten drawers and cupboards. In the seventeenth century little posies of aromatic and scented dried leaves and flowers called tussie-mussies were carried to ward off the plague.

In the nineteenth century the imagination of the Victorians was captured by their great plant hunters who searched the world. Enthusiasts at home made wonderful collections of pressed flowers and leaves and made arrangements of dried flowers, grasses and rushes. Since then, interest in dried flowers has fluctuated, gradually waning, until by the early 1970s the selection of dried flowers available in flower shops was limited to just a few grasses, statice and straw-flowers, often dyed in violent colours.

Hang drying
We started to dry our own flowers in the ceiling space of our flower shop ten years ago with the idea of regaining and making available the great beauty that natural dried flowers have. Soon the ceiling was crammed, making the shop into a flower-filled cavern. We quickly found that hanging bunches of flowers to air dry was the easiest and most effective way of preserving them. We experimented, hanging up many common or garden flowers and foliage as well as the special flowers that we bought fresh from London's wonderful Covent Garden market.

We found we were able to preserve a much greater range of natural colours in the more usual drying flowers, such as statice, helichrysum and helipterum, than was available ready-dried, and we went on to establish a regular supply of dried roses, delphiniums and larkspur, astilbe, gypsophila and mimosa along with a host of other flowers, grasses, seedheads and leaves. The list has gone on expanding year after year, and with it an awakening interest that has now made dried flowers a growth industry. Commercial nurseries all over the world are growing flowers solely for drying, and a distribution network has been set up so that it is possible to buy ready-dried flowers that are native to many far flung countries.

Other drying techniques
Although we have found air drying to be the simplest and most effective method, you will see that there are several other ways that plant material can be

A range of tones
An ancient cane-bound stoneware oil
jar overflows with flowers, ranging
from deep reds on the left to pale pinks
on the right. Flowers used include
roses, larkspur, helichrysum, alliums,
feather flower, reeds and a silvery
coloured protea.

preserved. Chemical dessicants and sand can be used to draw the moisture content from plant material. This method is not as easy to carry out as air drying, but if you have the patience it can provide you with some very beautiful flowers that, although rather brittle, retain much of their natural fresh colour and texture. Roses, paeonies, Christmas roses, lilies, orchids, tulips and zinnias are particularly well-preserved when dried in this way.

Then you will find that glycerine can be used to replace the moisture content of many leaves and a few flowers. In this way the plants retain their suppleness, but mostly change their colours to become rather heavy and lifeless. We feel that only eucalyptus and bells-of-Ireland (*Moluccella* sp.) are really attractive preserved in this way.

Pressing flowers and foliage between sheets of absorbent paper is another method of drying you will find in this book. Like chemical drying, this method produces good colour retention, but the resulting material is completely flat and therefore not so useful for arrangements, but needs rather to be mounted, framed and glazed to be shown to best advantage.

The pleasures of arranging

The exciting process of growing and drying flowers yourself, or simply buying bunches of dried flowers at a flower shop is just the beginning of the creative

process of arranging them and this is at once tremendously enjoyable and therapeutic – any worries will soon be completely forgotten as you begin to make your dried flower arrangements.

Although we hope that this book will be helpful in showing the techniques that lead to making an arrangement we have to say that there are no rules for arranging flowers, no lists of dried flowers that look particularly well together, no definitive combinations of colours that work better than others. Rather, nature must give us the leads required when creating with flowers. The sort of formality that is often seen in both fresh and dried flower arrangements seldom plays a part in this process.

Our aim is to show a wide range of plant material that can be grown and dried and then to present some of the ways that we have chosen to arrange this material, frequently taking our inspiration from the way that plants grow and the shapes they make in the landscape. Some of the arrangements are simple, while those for special or festive occasions are more complex. They all have a wild character that reflects our particular style.

Everyone needs a little inspiration to develop their creativity and we hope that we can hand on to you some of the inspiration that has enabled us to produce this book, in addition to showing you the basic skills required for drying and arranging dried flowers.

Delicate arrangement (left)
This arrangement of honesty, gypsophila, cornflowers, tiny red roses, larkspur and helipterum beautifully complements the glass bowl lined with shimmering silver and scraps of coloured paper.

Overhead view (right)
This wicker basket is crammed full of field grasses interlaced with yellow helichrysum, anaphalis, helipterum, achillea and silene. It makes a dramatic arrangement when viewed from above.

If you are fortunate enough to have a garden, however small or large, it is relatively easy to grow some plants that you can harvest, dry and use to make arrangements for yourself and your friends. Undertaking the complete process of growing, preserving and arranging enables you to enjoy the plants both living and dried, and is an altogether rewarding experience. The scale that you grow on is unimportant. It is just as rewarding to dry a few mixed bunches as to fill a whole ceiling space with hanging bunches of flowers that you have grown. In a small garden of no more than 6 × 9 m (20 × 30 ft), it is quite possible to grow enough material to make three or four large dried flower arrangements, without seriously affecting the look of the garden as you harvest. In larger gardens you can produce more material in proportion to this estimate.

Garden planning
That flowers for drying have to be picked just before they reach perfection is an important consideration when it comes to planning your garden with dried plants in mind. Every garden should be attractive for as much of the year as possible and you will not want it to look denuded as you harvest all the ready-to-open flower buds. In any garden border it is the juxtaposition of plants with contrasted shapes, different sized and textured leaves (some being deciduous, some evergreen), and differently shaped flowers in various combinations of colours, that make for interest and intrigue. So the beds in your garden need to have a mixture of plants established according to a plan that will not be affected appreciably by the removal of some flowers and foliage for drying.

The border is an area of flower bed that most people with a garden possess. It can be a strip of soil maybe only a metre wide, often bounded by a fence, wall or hedge on one side and grass on the other. Herbaceous borders (devoted solely to perennial plants that die back in winter) are not nearly as fashionable as they were and the mixed border has taken their place. These contain some herbaceous plants but also decorative shrubs, climbers and boundary shrubs, roses and annuals, all in a glorious mixture. Such mixed borders provide interest over a long period, especially if they are well planned. They are ideal sites for a good selection of plants for drying, such as hardy perennials and annuals, which can be interspersed with flowering shrubs and roses to great effect.

If you have an existing border of shrubs mixed with perennials that does not contain enough material for drying, you can re-structure it to make way for more in winter when the existing herbaceous perennials are dormant. Mark the position of these plants before they die down. Leaving any major shrubs that are in good positions, split up the existing herbaceous plants that are in large clumps and make room for pockets of additional perennials for drying as well as some annuals, which you can grow from seed and plant out in spring or early summer as directed on the seed packet. Many rushes and ferns, which provide fronds, stems and seedheads, essential decoration in many dried flower arrangements, tend to prefer very damp soil and are therefore best grown in a separate area of the garden (see p.15).

Choosing plants
Whether starting from scratch or re-organizing beds, it is worthwhile mapping out a planting plan on paper, detailing the height and width of the mature plants you choose together with their flower and foliage colours and month of flowering. Sticking to a colour scheme is very important, both in large and small gardens. Use the colours that you like boldly, but beware of making the range of colours too wide, especially in small gardens. If you intend adding plant colour to an existing bed, aim to make the colours of the flowers you are going to plant relate to the existing planting scheme.

There is a relatively small number of plants ideal both for a sunny border site, and for partial cutting to remove a proportion of the flowers or leaves for drying, bearing in mind that the border should continue to look full and interesting.

Among perennial plants for well-drained soil of around neutral acidity/alkalinity, there are lavender, achillea (which is now available in yellow, white and pink), roses of all colours, hybrid delphiniums, paeonies (for the large garden only as they have such a short flowering period), alliums, poppies, decorative thistles, gypsophila and solidago. All these are best planted in groups rather than as single plants.

Annuals for drying are also best grown in groups. There is a startling colour range of strawflowers (*Helichrysym bracteatum*), a native of Australia and probably best-known of the "everlasting" flowers. They can be white, cream-pink, lilac, bright yellow, brilliant red and orange and it is understandable that these have always been popular as dried flowers even if their stems are a little weak. There are many varieties of statice (*Limonium* sp.). Again the colour range is huge and it is possible to buy seed according to colour. *Limonium suworowii* is well worth growing for its spikes of rosy-pink flowers in summer. Helipterums and xeranthemums in pinks and whites, larkspur in shades of blue, pink and white – all of these annuals

Border garden (above)
With a larger garden you can afford the luxury of having wide mixed borders. Here a path winds its way nonchalantly between beds that contain a wide variety of plants, many of which can be dried for flowers, seedheads and foliage. At the beginning of summer, these borders will yield plentiful yellow and white achillea, delphiniums, and alchemilla for drying.

Summery basket (right)
This large, summery basket is arranged with dried *Achillea ptarmica*, *Achillea filipendulina*, alchemilla and delphiniums and could easily be mistaken for a work basket filled with freshly gathered flowers.

create beautiful areas of colour and will flower throughout the summer months. All of them can be air dried (see pp.170–173) extremely easily.

Plants for shade

In some cases, an area of a garden, or indeed a whole garden, receives little or no sunshine, either because it has high walls or because it is shaded by trees or nearby houses. There are not so many plants that can be grown in these shady positions that will dry well, but the few that do are well worth trying. Again, it is the overall look of the garden throughout the year that counts and the harvesting of material for drying should be seen as a bonus.

Ferns certainly love to grow in shady places and there are many species that grow into very attractive shapes and sizes. Some of them are even evergreen. All the leaves of ferns dry extremely well by pressing. For a large garden space *Osmunda regalis* is magnificent. In favourable conditions (this fern likes to have "damp feet") it will provide fronds 1.5 m (5 ft) long. *Matteucia struthiopteris* also grows tall and so do the male and female ferns, *Dryopteris filix-mas* and *Athyrium filix-femina*. Evergreen ferns that are well worth growing are *Blechnum tabulare*, *Phyllitis scolopendrium* and *Polystichum setiferum*.

Some other shade-loving plants that will dry are: hostas, both for their leaves and seedheads; a few roses, such as the climbers 'The New Dawn' and 'Zéphrin Drouhin'; camellias, the leaves of which can be glycerined while their flowers are dried with dessicants; bamboos, mahonias, the Mexican orange blossom (*Choisya ternata*) and hellebores.

Ivies are excellent climbers for shady walls or fences and there are beautiful varieties such as *Hedera colchica dentata aurea* with its gold-splashed leaves, the silvery forms of Canary ivy, *Hedera canariensis*, and varieties of the small-leaved *Hedera helix*, such as 'Goldheart' and 'Glacier'. Once established these will cover large areas with their beautiful evergreen leaves. They can also be used as ground cover but have to be kept in check as they root wherever their stems touch the earth. Ivy strands can be glycerined or their leaves pressed. Evergreen honeysuckle *Lonicera halliana* can also be rampageous, but it grows well in shade and its very sweetly scented flowers, produced from late spring onwards, can be used in pot-pourri.

Plants for semi-shade

Although violas will not tolerate total shade they will grow and flower profusely in a semi-shaded place. The same can be said for hydrangeas. They require a moisture-retaining soil to produce their sumptuous

flower-heads. It is important to harvest them at the right time, when the little true flower at the centre of each bract has just withered. It is better to pick them late rather than too early. There are many varieties to choose from, but the true blues need an acid soil to retain their colour year after year, otherwise they will turn pink or green. *Alchemilla mollis* is a small herbaceous plant with beautiful, fan-shaped leaves and frothy golden flowers. It will grow in a semi-shaded position and will spread rapidly by seeding itself. Both leaves and flowers dry well. Astilbe requires the same conditions to throw up its delicate spires of flowers. There are rust, pink, cream and white varieties and they air dry easily.

Compartmentalized gardens

A garden divided into compartments has a great sense of excitement and mystery, and provides a layout that suits growing for drying particularly well. A compartment can be put aside as a cutting garden with rows of plants set out like a vegetable garden. Here, flowers for drying such as lavender, strawflowers, helipterums, physalis, achillea, larkspur and roses, and maybe vegetables and flowers for fresh cutting can be grown. The overall garden need not be large, in fact not much larger than a room for each compartment. Like rooms in houses the various spaces can have different atmospheres, different colour schemes, and

Shady arrangement (left)
Dryopteris and osmunda fern leaves form the basis of this autumn-looking arrangement, which also includes hosta leaves and hellebore leaves and flowers. The mixture sets off the antique Chinese brass bowl perfectly, with some tiny bright red *Rosa* 'Paleander', picked from a sunnier position, added for extra interest.

Shady garden (right)
You can grow plenty of material for drying in a shaded patch of a garden or courtyard. Ferns grow extremely well in the shade and mahonia, choisya and ivies also do well. Hellebore and hosta are ideal for growing in shady gardens and their leaves can be pressed easily, while the seedheads of hostas can be air-dried and the flowers of hellebores can be dried using dessicants.

can be furnished with plants that have thematic associations. A terrace can be formal, maybe separated from another area by a hedge, and in the second part of the garden the plantings can have a wild cottage feel. Another garden compartment could be composed of silver-leaved plants, interspersed with groups of cool-coloured flowering plants. *Senecio greyi*, artemisia and santolina all dry well and look very attractive in the garden. Rosemary and lavender also have silvery leaves, but lavender flowers dry better than the foliage and dried rosemary is more useful for culinary rather than decorative purposes.

Ornamental grasses are beautiful plants to grow and could occupy a compartment. They need a well-drained situation and prefer a sunny or half-sunny bed. Both their spiky leaves and seedheads are extremely decorative and a group of them in a border can make an interesting feature. Some grow large,

Silver arrangement
(above)
An iridescent oval vase requires a sparkling arrangement to complement it. A subtle mix of *Senecio greyi* leaves, *Stachys lanata* flower-heads, white hydrangea heads, white roses and tiny blue larkspur sprays laced with little bunches of lavender flowers proves the perfect combination.

Silver border
(right)
A planting of many silver-leaved plants with white roses and hydrangeas and some groups of blue larkspur yields plenty of material for drying in this compartmentalized garden. *Senecio greyi*, santolinas, artemisias and stachys dry well.

Garden of grasses (right)
Grasses are particulary strong in their growing form, with their long leaves and intriguing seedhead sprays. They must be regularly divided to keep them in check, and to keep each clump attractively bushy.

Arrangement of grasses (below)
This arrangement uses a wide selection of dried grasses to complement the basket. Pampas, reeds, cob corn, oats, quaking grass, lagurus and carex form the basis of this dried arrangement, while some spiky solidago, sprays of stirlingia and lotus seeds add to the range of colours and textures.

such as pampas grass (*Cortaderia selloana*), which sends up flowering stems 2.75–3 m (9–10 ft) tall and eventually becomes 2 m (6½ ft) wide at the base. Species of *Miscanthus*, *Scirpus* and *Carex* and, as ground cover, *Luzula* and *Festuca*, are all decorative as well as providing good material for drying. Most of these grasses can become invasive and must be kept in check by frequent division. Being vigorous growers they can be cropped regularly for drying through the growing season.

If you have a naturally boggy area in your garden you might like to grow bog-loving plants there and make a feature of the area.

Roses
Rose blooms have an unparalleled beauty, both in the shape and arrangement of petals and in the delicious scent that many varieties possess. They make excellent drying material, although the multi-petalled varieties are more suitable for air drying than the single roses.

The past three hundred years have given us an enormous variety of roses to choose from and catalogues from both general and specialist nurseries list hundreds of different roses, so much so that the choice can be bewildering. Recently, nurseries have been producing new roses that combine the shape and scent of the old ones, such as damasks and gallicas, with a perpetual flowering habit, a great advantage for the flower arranger. The resistance of the leaves to black spot and mildew has also been substantially improved. Examples include: 'Heritage' (pale pink), 'Mary Rose' (bright pink), 'Graham Thomas' (yellow), 'Bredon' (buff), 'Dove' (blush white) and 'The Squire' (deep red). Study the opening buds of your roses and cut stems or heads for drying an estimated four days before the blooms come to perfection.

Rose plants are at their best grown in groups in a border or, if the space is available, in a complete rose garden, which can look marvellous right through the summer and early autumn. In small beds, the blooms look well set off by silvery foliage. You might try interspersing them with silver-leaved santolinas and lavenders. If you have little space, consider clothing a wall or fence with a climbing or rambling rose.

Rose arrangement (above)
A pretty pink and blue glazed vase is filled with a delicate arrangement of bright pink roses and dried white broom.

Rose garden (below)
Here, *Rosa gallica maxima* produces huge quantities of flowers in early summer. Its petals are especially useful for pot-pourris.

INGREDIENTS

The following pages are a colour-by-colour guide to the dried flowers and plants that make the ingredients of arrangements. Some plants, such as statice (*Limonium* sp.), roses (*Rosa* sp.) and everlasting flowers (*Helichrysum* sp.), are invaluable since they grow in a profusion of different forms and colours. The ingredients illustrated are widely available, although they originate from many regions of the world. A few of them (some cones and leaves) were gathered from the wild with great care, so as not to damage the parent plant. Never take protected nor endangered wild plant material.

REDS & PINKS

Radiant and glorious reds and pinks are redolent of summer, the colours we associate with great borders of flowers hazy in the afternoon sun. These colours bring loud fanfares to mind, yet they also recall the pale but brilliant wash that suffuses the sky at dawn or dusk.

The reds top the colour temperature chart; they are rich and darkly majestic, but violent too. Red is the colour of the most sweetly scented roses and the most spectacular tropical flowers. Reds can be regal, exotic and powerful, or they can be brash and overblown.

Pinks are a little cooler, though still high on the temperature scale. At their most flamboyant they can

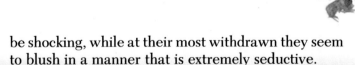

be shocking, while at their most withdrawn they seem to blush in a manner that is extremely seductive.

Many roses appear in this particular colour range and you might be surprised at their similarity to freshly cut blooms. They are, in fact, very easy to dry if picked about four days before the blooms reach perfection. They should be air-dried, hanging in bunches, with the heads kept well apart (see pp.170–173). The drying process tends to darken the tone of red roses and fade the tone of pink roses.

Rich summery combination
This glowing combination
of summer flowers features
pink paeonies that have
been dried chemically.
These are offset by red
roses, delicate bunches of
silene, deeper pink onion
heads and acacia foliage.
The pewter container, with
its bulbous shape and raised
flower design, inspired this
fan-shaped arrangement.

Pink fescue grass
Festuca sp.

Honesty
Lunaria rediviva

Brome grass
Bromus sp.

Pink cardoon
Cynara sp.

Onion
Allium sp.

Hair-grass
Aira sp.

Protea or
Cape honey flower
Protea compacta

Pennisetum *Pennisetum* sp.

**Pale pink
fescue grass**
Festuca sp.

Australian honeysuckle
Banksia occidentalis

Common quaking grass
Briza media

Australian honeysuckle
Banksia menziesii

Paeony
Paeonia lactiflora

**Mop-headed
hydrangea**
Hydrangea macrophylla

Hair-grass
Aira sp.

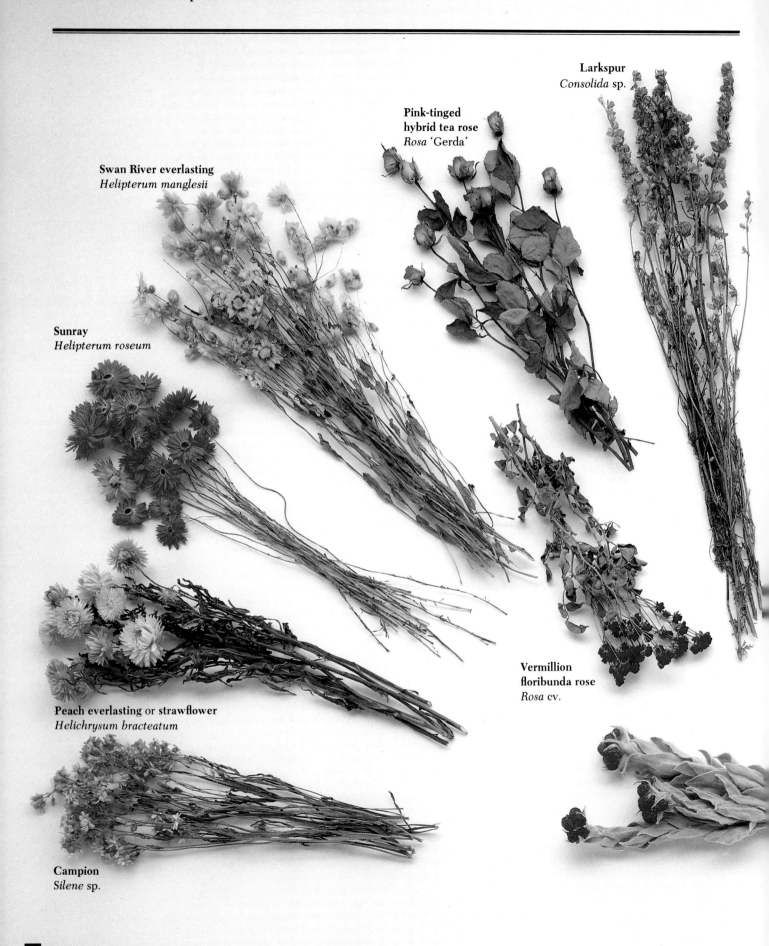

Larkspur
Consolida sp.

**Pink-tinged
hybrid tea rose**
Rosa 'Gerda'

Swan River everlasting
Helipterum manglesii

Sunray
Helipterum roseum

**Vermillion
floribunda rose**
Rosa cv.

Peach everlasting or **strawflower**
Helichrysum bracteatum

Campion
Silene sp.

Red bottlebrush
Callistemon beaufortia sparsa

**Cerise-tinged
hybrid tea rose**
Rosa 'Mercedes'

Salmon-pink statice
Limonium sp.

Sunray
Helipterum sp.

Globe amaranth
Gomphrena globosa

**Terracotta
miniature rose**
Rosa cv.

Phaenocoma shrub
Phaenocoma prolifera

Silver strawberry
Leptospermum sp.

Bell heather
Erica cinerea

**Rich red everlasting
or strawflower**
*Helichrysum
bracteatum*

**Button snakeroot, blazing star
or Kansas gayfeather**
Liatris spicata

**Deep scarlet
hybrid tea rose**
Rosa 'Ilona'

Russian or rat's tail statice
Limonium suworowii

Celastrus
Celastrus sp.

Copper beech
Fagus sylvatica 'Cuprea'

**Deep red everlasting
or strawflower**
*Helichrysum
bracteatum*

Yarrow
Achillea millefolium

Pom-pom dahlia
Dahlia sp.

**Scarlet-tinged
hybrid tea rose**
Rosa 'Jaguar'

Red kangaroo paw
*Anigozanthos
rufus*

Celosia cockscomb
Celosia argentea cristata

Leucodendron
Leucodendron sp.

Bronze-leaved eucalyptus
Eucalyptus sp.

ORANGES & YELLOWS

Lying next to each other in the colour spectrum, both orange and yellow have powerful qualities. Yellow is closely associated with the spring and radiates a sense of new growth and freshness. The bright yellow flowers that can be dried will always give a sparkle of liveliness to arrangements, although the flowers themselves (with the exception of mimosa) are not spring flowers at all – most of them flower during the summer months.

Orange has a liveliness of another kind, a glowing strength. It has strong associations with harvest and the mellow warmth of late summer. Think of the richness of a sun-dried corn head, for example. Orange and yellow, and their golden and apricot intermediary tones, group together to form arrangements that are vibrant and full of sunshine.

There are some strong, bright yellows to be found amongst the many varieties of helichrysum, statice and achillea, and orange is very well represented again by helichrysum and by the glowing lanterns of physalis. All of these are best air-dried, hanging in bunches (see pp.170–173), although with physalis you must be careful to remove the leaves on the stems where the bunches are tied, to avoid rotting.

A fruit that is well worth growing for its decorative qualities alone is the gourd. Gourds are a great bonus to the dried flower arranger in late autumn, providing beautiful yellow and orange specimens in particular. Gourd plants need plenty of summer sunshine to produce an abundant crop, but if you are lucky with the weather, the gourds you cut will keep for many months in a dry atmosphere. The application of a coat of household varnish can help to prolong the life of a gourd, although the sheen produced can sometimes look unnatural.

Glowing arrangement
The basket used in this
arrangement is designed to
hold a dozen bottles of wine,
but here it carries a selection
of separate bunches of dried
flowers in its compartments.
Orange and yellow
helichrysum, apricot-
coloured statice, mimosa,
some Chinese lanterns,
carthamus and Jerusalem
sage create an eye-catching
arrangement, full of warmth
and energy.

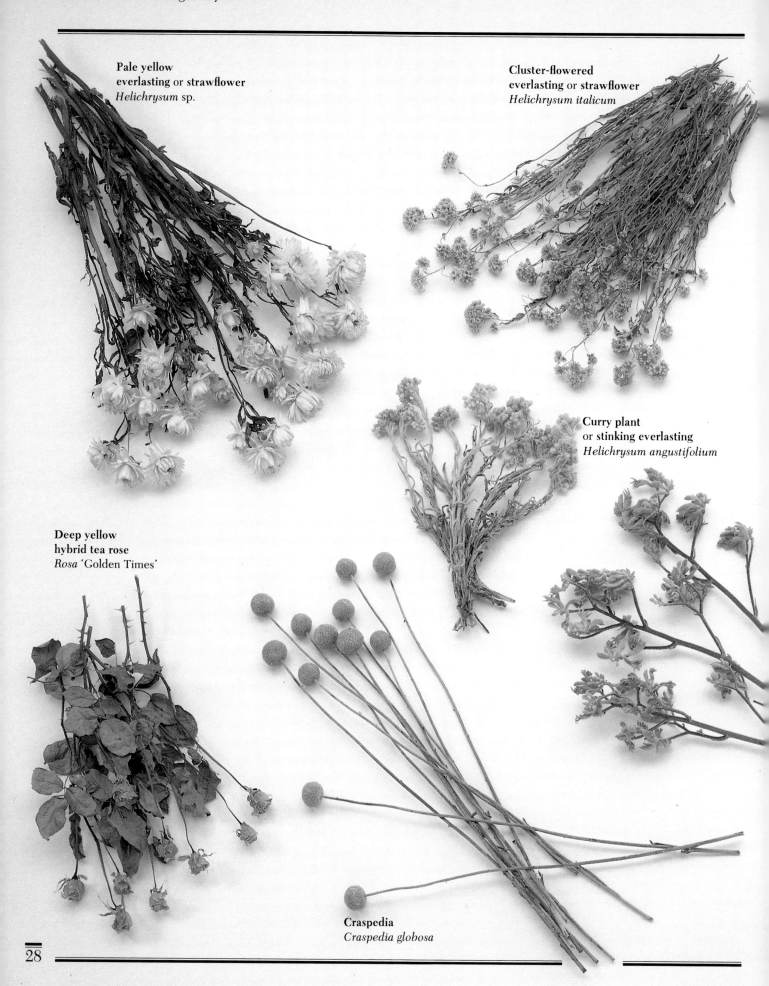

**Pale yellow
everlasting** or **strawflower**
Helichrysum sp.

**Cluster-flowered
everlasting** or **strawflower**
Helichrysum italicum

Curry plant
or **stinking everlasting**
Helichrysum angustifolium

**Deep yellow
hybrid tea rose**
Rosa 'Golden Times'

Craspedia
Craspedia globosa

**Golden
everlasting** or **strawflower**
Helichrysum sp.

Deep yellow yarrow
Achillea filipendulina
'Coronation Gold'

**Bronze-tinged
hybrid tea rose**
Rosa 'La Minuette'

Sunray
Helipterum sp.

Yellow kangaroo paw
Anigozanthos sp.

**Silver-leaved
everlasting** or **strawflower**
Helichrysum sp.

Australian honeysuckle
Banksia baxteri

Tansy
Chrysanthemum sp.

Lady's mantle
Alchemilla mollis

African daisies
Arctosis sp.

Mimosa or **wattle**
Acacia sp.

Golden-flowered statice
Limonium sp.

Jerusalem sage
Phlomis fruticosa

Golden rod
Solidago canadensis

Golden yarrow
Achillea sp.

Feather flower
Verticordia sp.

Dryandra
Dryandra quercifolia

Australian honeysuckle
Banksia attenuata

Light golden yarrow
Achillea sp.

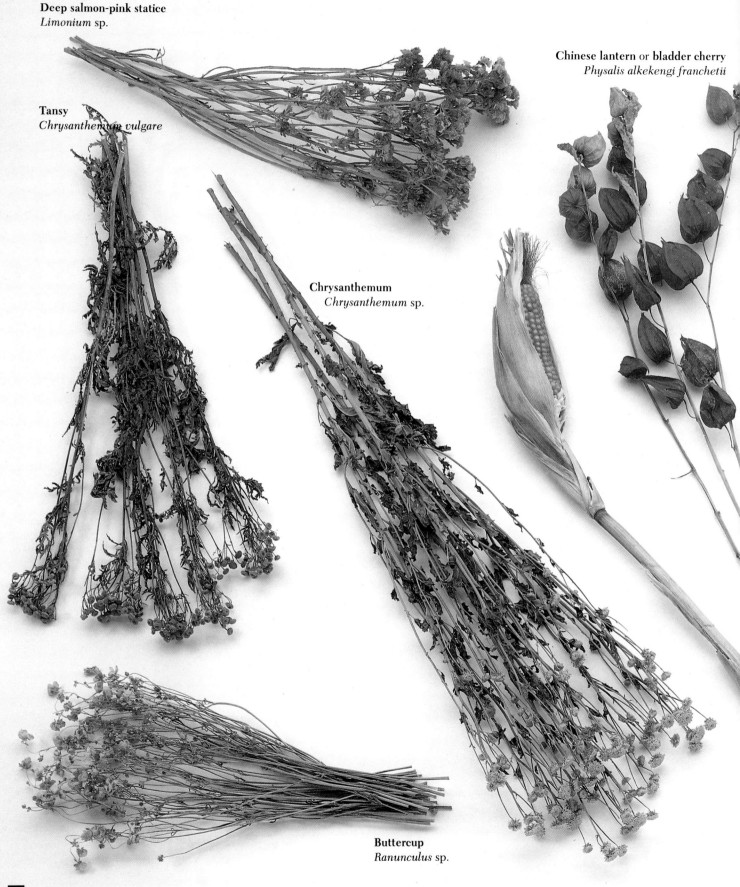

Deep salmon-pink statice
Limonium sp.

Chinese lantern or **bladder cherry**
Physalis alkekengi franchetii

Tansy
Chrysanthemum vulgare

Chrysanthemum
Chrysanthemum sp.

Buttercup
Ranunculus sp.

Safflower or **dyer's saffron**
Carthamus tinctorius

Pot marigold
Calendula officinalis

Dock or **sorrel**
Rumex sp.

**Orange-yellow
hybrid tea rose**
Rosa cv.

Small-headed yarrow
Achillea sp.

Sweet corn (fruit)
Zea mays

GREENS & BROWNS

Green and brown might be called the true colours of nature. They predominate in the countryside and are present, in varying tones and differing amounts, throughout all the seasons.

Greens that defy imitation by the painter's brush fill the summer landscape. Green is the colour of leaves and grasses. It signifies growth. The dazzlingly brilliant lime green of fresh meadow grass and young foliage moderates to a less brilliant green as plants mature. As summer ripens, trees and hedgerows become a rich green foil to grassland and sky. Green can, however, have a sombre tone, in forests for example, or on moors or mountainsides.

Because there is so much of it, green is a colour that most of us take for granted. Even the densest cities contain a surprising amount of it, whether it is in gardens, in tree-lined streets or in parks.

In general, dried foliage and grasses do not retain the brilliant fresh green of new growth but become softly muted in colour. Nearly all leaves can be pressed, but, although they retain their colour in this form, their flatness makes them less easy to use in arrangements. There is sufficient variety of air-dried leaves available to give arrangements the natural look that becomes them so well.

Brown is the colour of wood, cones, seeds and the soil itself. It tends naturally to be associated with winter, the season when trees become brown outlines against the stark grey sky, and in the countryside great areas of tilled soil fill the landscape.

Seedheads, cones, cereals and reeds, autumn foliage with its rich browns and the bare branches and twigs of winter, all these can be dried most successfully. The variety of their shapes can be used to make the basic structure of a multitude of arrangements.

Wheatfield arrangement
A wooden box that once contained tomatoes has been used for this arrangement. Moss, lichen, cones, eucalyptus seeds and dried fungi have been stuck to all the visible surfaces. The interior of the box is filled with foam that is covered with a thin layer of Indian moss. Rows of wheat stems are easily arranged in the foam and the space between the stems scattered with cones and seeds.

Textural arrangement
A hollow piece of lichen-covered bark is the container for an arrangement of dryandra leaves, love-in-a-mist seed pods, alyssum seedheads and some green statice. Like the simple arrangement of cereal stems, right, this has a natural country look.

Pin oak
Quercus palustris

Big or **large
quaking grass**
Briza maxima

Lesser or **small
quaking grass**
Briza minima

Lime
Tilia sp.

Dill
*Anethum
graveolens*

Clubrush
Scirpus sp.

Bamboo
Arundinaria sp.

Banksia
Banksia sp.

Six-rowed barley
Hordeum vulgare

Reed canary grass
Phalaris arundinacea

Big or large quaking grass
Briza maxima

Panicled hydrangea
Hydrangea paniculata

Mop-headed hydrangea
Hydrangea macrophylla

Timothy
Phleum pratense

Rough bristle grass
Setaria verticillata

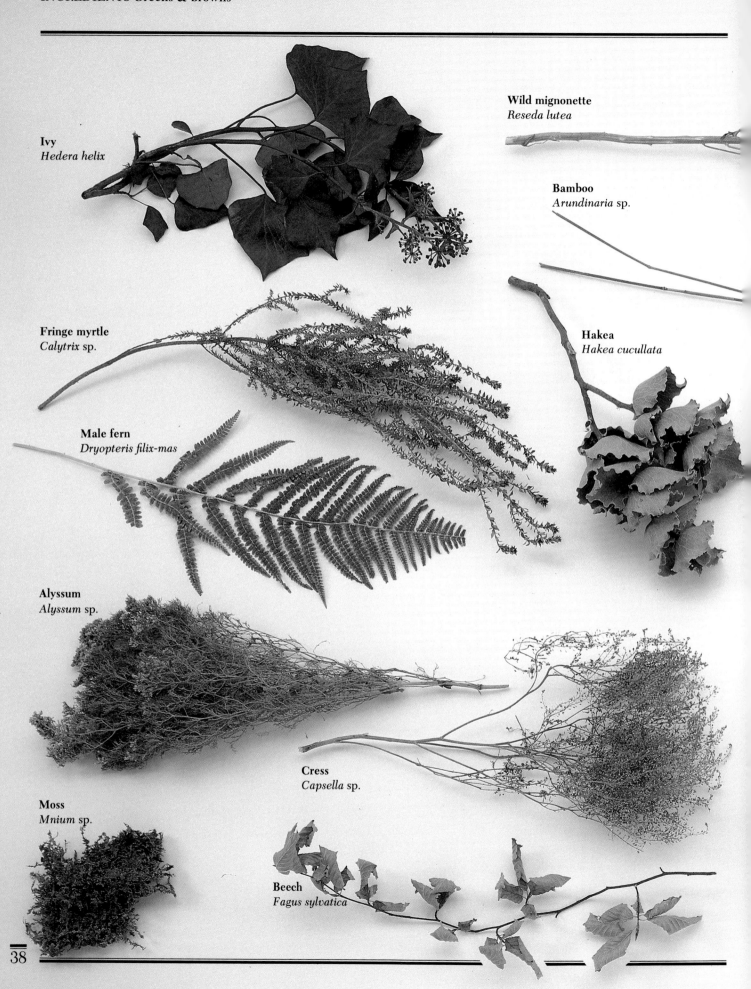

Ivy
Hedera helix

Wild mignonette
Reseda lutea

Bamboo
Arundinaria sp.

Fringe myrtle
Calytrix sp.

Hakea
Hakea cucullata

Male fern
Dryopteris filix-mas

Alyssum
Alyssum sp.

Cress
Capsella sp.

Moss
Mnium sp.

Beech
Fagus sylvatica

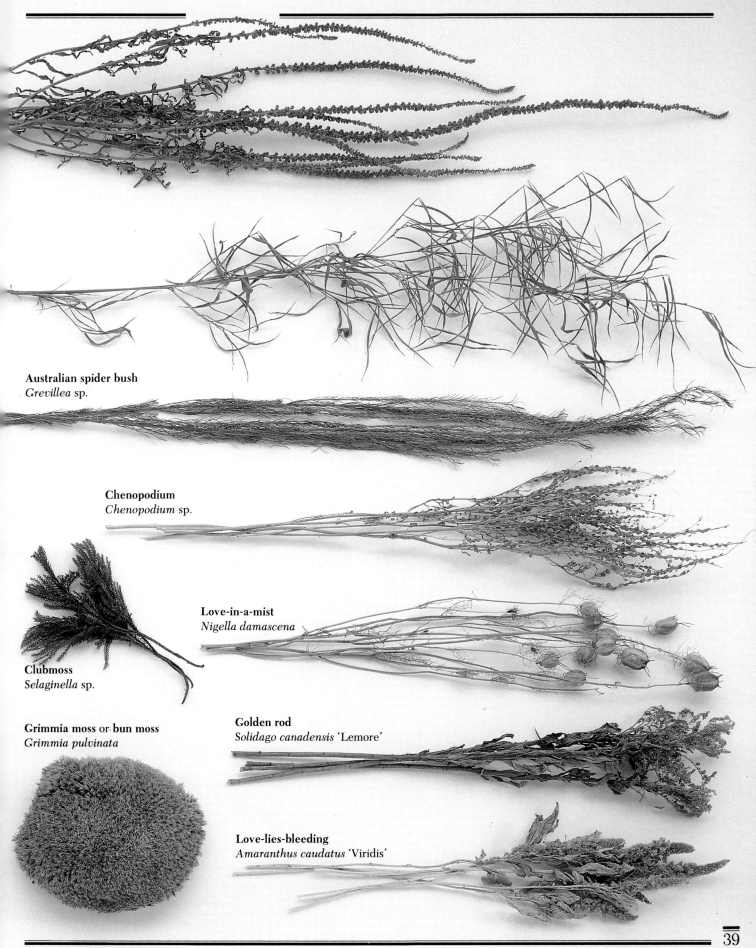

Australian spider bush
Grevillea sp.

Chenopodium
Chenopodium sp.

Clubmoss
Selaginella sp.

Love-in-a-mist
Nigella damascena

Grimmia moss or bun moss
Grimmia pulvinata

Golden rod
Solidago canadensis 'Lemore'

Love-lies-bleeding
Amaranthus caudatus 'Viridis'

Snow gum
Eucalyptus niphophila

Scots pine
Pinus sylvestris

Rush
Juncus sp.

Dryandra
Dryandra sp.

Mop-headed hydrangea
Hydrangea macrophylla

Leucodendron
Leucodendron sp.

Reed
Phragmites australis

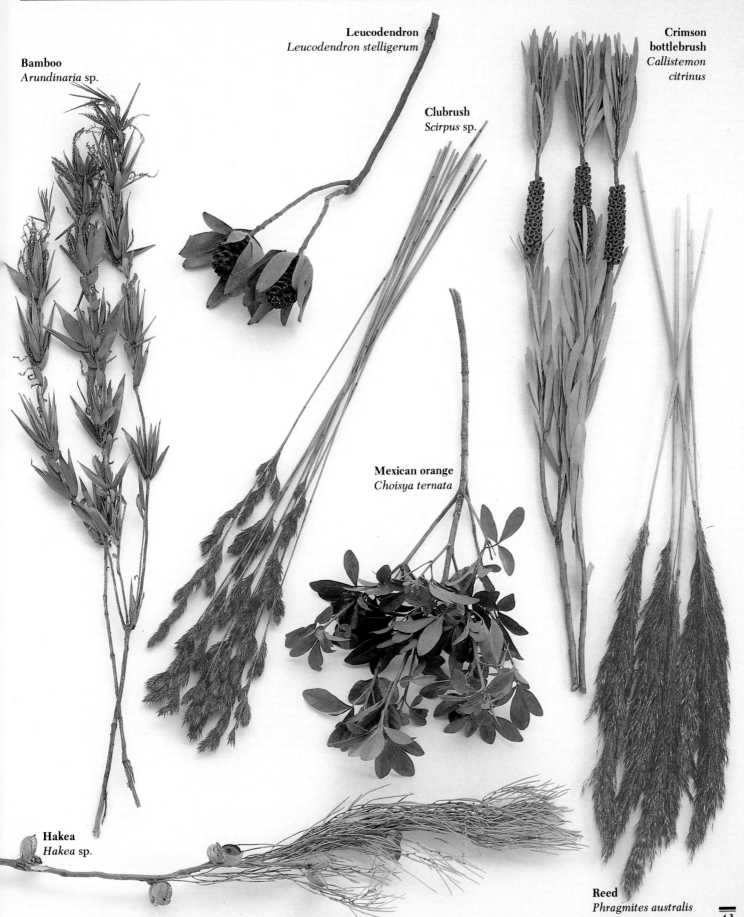

Bamboo
Arundinaria sp.

Leucodendron
Leucodendron stelligerum

Clubrush
Scirpus sp.

**Crimson
bottlebrush**
*Callistemon
citrinus*

Mexican orange
Choisya ternata

Hakea
Hakea sp.

Reed
Phragmites australis

Black-eared barley
Hordeum sp.

Greater reedmace
Typha latifolia

Rattan palm or **wait-awhile vine**
Calamus sp.

Paradise nut or **sapucia nut**
Lecythis usitata

Lesser reedmace
Typha angustifolia

Pine cone
Pinus sp.

Tolbos or **top-brush**
Leucodendron rubrum

Mugwort
Artemisia vulgaris

Mexican white pine cone
Pinus ayacahuite

Scots pine cone
Pinus sylvestris

Larch cone
Larix sp.

Pin oak
Quercus palustris

Lotus flower (fruit)
Nelumbo lucifera

Silver birch
Betula pendula

Reed
Phragmites australis

Millet
Milium sp.

Globe artichoke
Cynara scolymus

Love-in-a-mist
Nigella damascena

Ornamental onion
Allium aflatunense

Hop
Humulus lupulus

Egyptian paper rush or **papyrus**
Cyperus papyrus

Fescue grass
Festuca sp.

Sedge
Carex sp.

Physocarpus
Physocarpus sp.

Leucodendron
Leucodendron sp.

BLUES & PURPLES

These are the withdrawn colours at the cool end of the colour spectrum. Blue can be intensely cold – the colour of oceans and glaciers – but it is also the colour of a cloudless sky and can make you think of warm sunny days. Beware, for sky-blue is caused by the refraction of the sun's rays through tiny particles of ice in the earth's atmosphere. The attraction of blue in the summer is its coolness.

Purple is less cold. It is the colour of hazy distant views, of faded pomp and great age. It is a difficult colour to use in dried flower arranging as it tends to create a sombre effect, but its violet and plum tones make interesting combinations with the blue tones, turquoise and sky-blue.

There are not many dried flowers in this colour range but they are memorable. Cornflowers, delphiniums and larkspur dry well and retain rich colour. Blue and lilac hydrangeas also retain their colour well but they are difficult to dry. They need to be left on the growing shrub until the tiny true flowers at the centre of the coloured bracts shrivel. The heads should then be picked and dried by hanging (see p.172) or placed upright in a vase with a little water that is left to evaporate (see p.170). *Limonium sinuatum*, liatris and amaranthus give good strong purples, whereas lavender tends to lose its colour during drying and its flowers can easily drop.

Cool arrangement
This mix of many of the tones in the blue and purple range complements the spiral of blue and turquoise that twists down the trumpet-shaped vase. The flowers in this striking and rich arrangement include echinops, eryngium, statice and larkspur.

Miniature group
None of these intensely blue miniature vases is more than 2.5cm (1 in) high, but combined with miniature dried plant material, they make an eye-catching group.

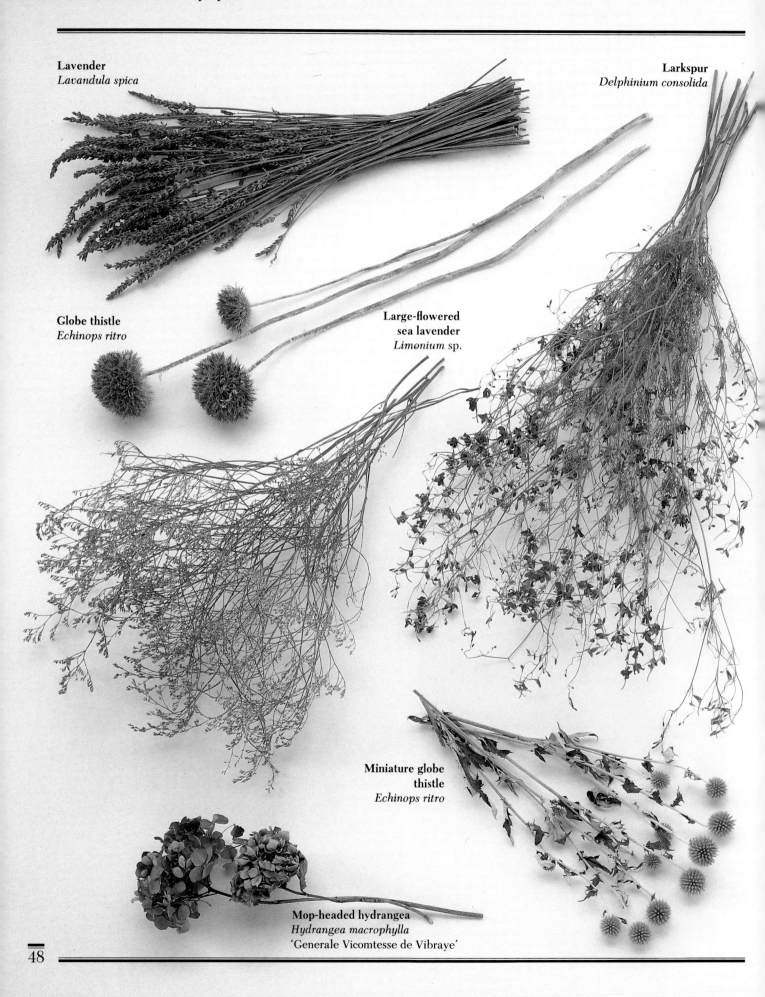

Lavender
Lavandula spica

Larkspur
Delphinium consolida

Globe thistle
Echinops ritro

**Large-flowered
sea lavender**
Limonium sp.

**Miniature globe
thistle**
Echinops ritro

Mop-headed hydrangea
Hydrangea macrophylla
'Generale Vicomtesse de Vibraye'

Eryngium
Eryngium sp.

Eryngium
Eryngium sp.

Sea lavender
Limonium sp.

Globe thistle
Echinops ritro

**Lilac-tinged
miniature rose**
Rosa 'Lilac Paleander'

**Blue-tinged
hydrangea florets**
Hydrangea macrophylla

Mauve statice
Limonium sinuatum

Perennial delphinium
Delphinium elatum cv.

Monkshood
Aconitum napellus

Love-lies-bleeding
Amaranthus sp.

Cornflower
Centaurea cyanus

Pink-purple statice
Limonium sinuatum

Purple statice
Limonium sinuatum

Small-flowered delphinium
Delphinium sp.

Astilbe
Astilbe davidii

Love-lies-bleeding
Amaranthus sp.

WHITE, CREAM & SILVER

This trio of colours as a whole represents purity, simplicity and elegance. White, the symbol of purity, however, can create a range of different moods. Together with yellow, it speaks of spring, the awakening of flowers and new life. As a foil to the jumble of riotous colours of summer, it provides a sense of calm and coolness. In complete contrast, white also epitomizes the bitter coldness of winter.

Cream is a colour that conveys a sense of great refinement – it is elegant, superior and distinctive. Like white, it is a good foil but it has a warmth that white does not possess. Silver, too, is a refined colour, reminding us of the pure and precious metal, but its grandeur is quiet and restrained.

Together, white, cream and silver produce arrangements of a light, almost transparent nature. This transparency is epitomized by the seedheads of honesty, only, however, after the two outer membranes of each seed case are peeled away to reveal the fine silvery interior disk (see p.179).

Both gypsophila and white rhodanthe retain their sparkling whiteness when they are air-dried. The best air-drying technique with gypsophila is to arrange the flowers in a vase with the stems in a small amount of water, which is then allowed to evaporate (see p.170).

**Muted harmony in
an arrangement**
This elegant arrangement,
in its pale wicker basket, is
composed of bunches of
many ingredients, including
carline thistles, hydrangeas,
helichrysum, moluccella,
gypsophila and honesty.

Tasmanian blue gum
Eucalyptus globulus

**Sea
lavender**
Limonium sp.

Pampas grass
Cortaderia selloana

Mimosa or
wattle
Acacia sp.

Senecio
Senecio greyi

Mullein
Verbascum sp.

Lamb's tongue
Stachys lanata

Melaleuca
Melaleuca sp.

**Miniature
cluster-flowered
everlasting**
Helichrysum sp.

**Miniature
everlasting**
*Pithocarpa
corymbulosa*

Bupleurum
Bupleurum sp.

**Silver-
flowered
everlastings**
*Cephalipterum
drummondii*

Common chamomile
Anthemis nobilis

Everlasting silver foliage
Helichrysum sp.

Stirlingia
Stirlingia latifolia

Daisy bush
Olearia sp.

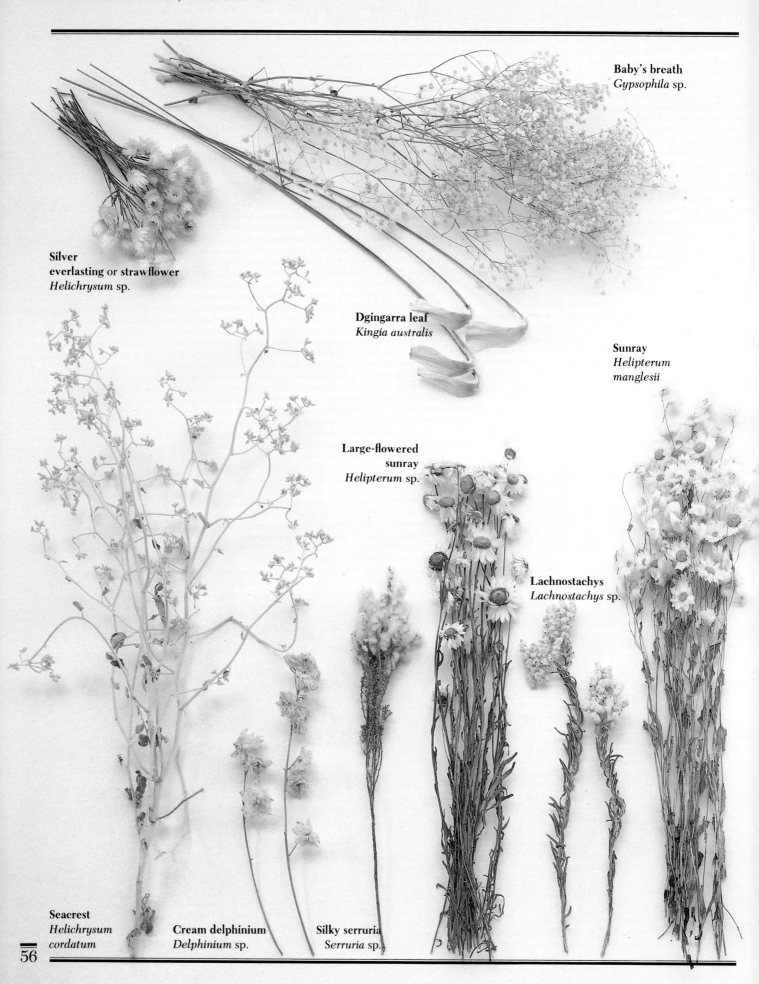

Baby's breath
Gypsophila sp.

**Silver
everlasting** or **strawflower**
Helichrysum sp.

Dgingarra leaf
Kingia australis

Sunray
*Helipterum
manglesii*

**Large-flowered
sunray**
Helipterum sp.

Lachnostachys
Lachnostachys sp.

Seacrest
*Helichrysum
cordatum*

Cream delphinium
Delphinium sp.

Silky serruria
Serruria sp.

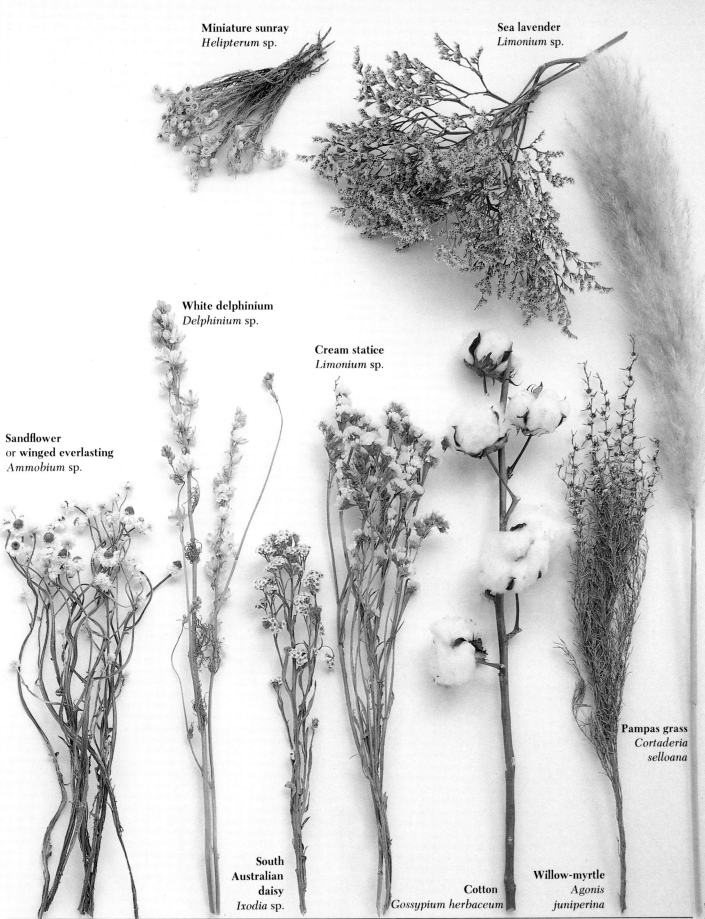

Miniature sunray
Helipterum sp.

Sea lavender
Limonium sp.

White delphinium
Delphinium sp.

Cream statice
Limonium sp.

Sandflower
or **winged everlasting**
Ammobium sp.

Pampas grass
Cortaderia
selloana

South
Australian
daisy
Ixodia sp.

Cotton
Gossypium herbaceum

Willow-myrtle
Agonis
juniperina

Woody pear
Xylomelum angustifolium

Bear's breeches
Acanthus spinosus

Stemless thistle
Carlina acaulis
'Caulescens'

Pink fruits
Dianthus sp.

Plantain lily (fruit)
Hosta sp.

Bells of Ireland or shell flower
Moluccella laevis

**White-flowering
hybrid tea rose**
Rosa
'Jack Frost'

Strawflower
*Helichrysum
bracteatum*

**Sphagnum
moss**
Sphagnum sp.

**Mop-headed
hydrangea**
*Hydrangea
macrophylla*

Nipplewort
Lapsana sp.

Onion
Allium sp.

Hogweed
Heracleum sphondylium

Chenopodium
Chenopodium sp.

Pampas grass
Cortaderia selloana

**Cluster-
flowered
sunray**
Helipterum sp.

Tassel flower
Cacalia sp.

**Field poppy
(fruit)**
Papaver rhoeas

**Feather
flower**
Verticordia sp.

**Grass
daisy**
Aphyllanthes sp.

**Sphagnum
moss**
Sphagnum sp.

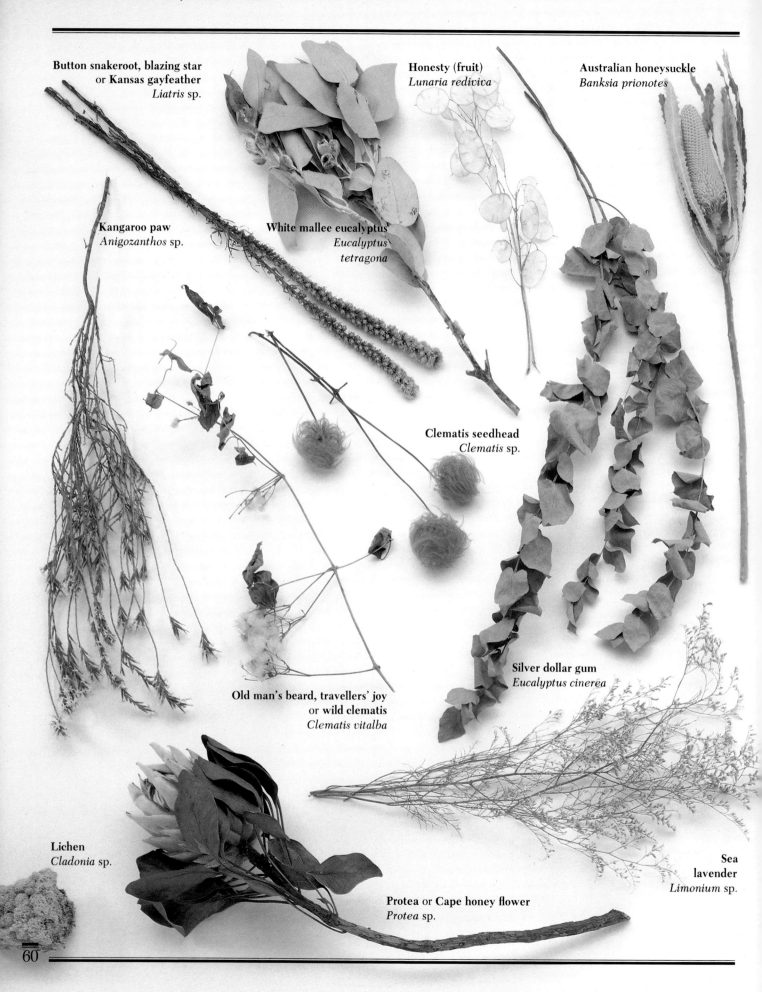

**Button snakeroot, blazing star
or Kansas gayfeather**
Liatris sp.

Honesty (fruit)
Lunaria rediviva

Australian honeysuckle
Banksia prionotes

Kangaroo paw
Anigozanthos sp.

White mallee eucalyptus
*Eucalyptus
tetragona*

Clematis seedhead
Clematis sp.

**Old man's beard, travellers' joy
or wild clematis**
Clematis vitalba

Silver dollar gum
Eucalyptus cinerea

Lichen
Cladonia sp.

**Sea
lavender**
Limonium sp.

Protea or **Cape honey flower**
Protea sp.

TOOLS MATERIALS & BASIC TECHNIQUES

The tools and materials required for making dried flower arrangements are few and simple. All you need is shown in this section, together with the necessary, though straightforward, techniques you should master to be sure of a professional finish. Become proficient at these techniques and you will be able to tackle the classic dried flower arrangements shown in the following chapter and feel confident of making up your own creations. Of vital importance in any arrangement is the container, so you will find a wide selection illustrated, together with ideas for modifying them to suit particular styles.

TOOLS & MATERIALS

There is a very wide range of equipment available to the professional flower arranger, but many items are useful only on the odd occasion. Set out below are the materials and tools most used for the arrangements that appear in this book. The essential items are high-quality florist's scissors, a tough steel knife and some dry foam. The other materials and tools are regularly useful and can be purchased at many flower shops or stores.

Cane
Cane can be used to lengthen or replace a heavy-headed flower stem to support it.

Glue
A fast-drying, clear-based glue is useful for sticking dried plant materials together or to containers, or for fixing dry foam to a container.

Glue

Adhesive tape

Dry-foam block

Dry-foam spheres

Dry foam
This is commercially available in several shapes. The brick is most useful, and can be cut to shape as required.

Adhesive clay

Adhesive clay
Adhesive clay comes in a roll and sticks well to non-porous and shiny surfaces.

Florist's spikes
These small plastic spikes are used to secure dry foam in bowls.

Chicken-wire

Florist's spikes

Adhesive tape
Tape, sticky on one side, binds dry foam well.

Plaster-of-Paris powder
Mixed with water, plaster-of-Paris powder dries to form a cheap medium for weighting top-heavy arrangements.

Chicken-wire
It is convenient to buy fine wire mesh 30-cm (1-ft) wide in a roll. It is used for bases and stem supports.

Setting clay
More expensive than plaster-of-Paris but easier to work, setting clay is also used to weight containers.

Plaster-of-Paris powder

Setting clay

Stones

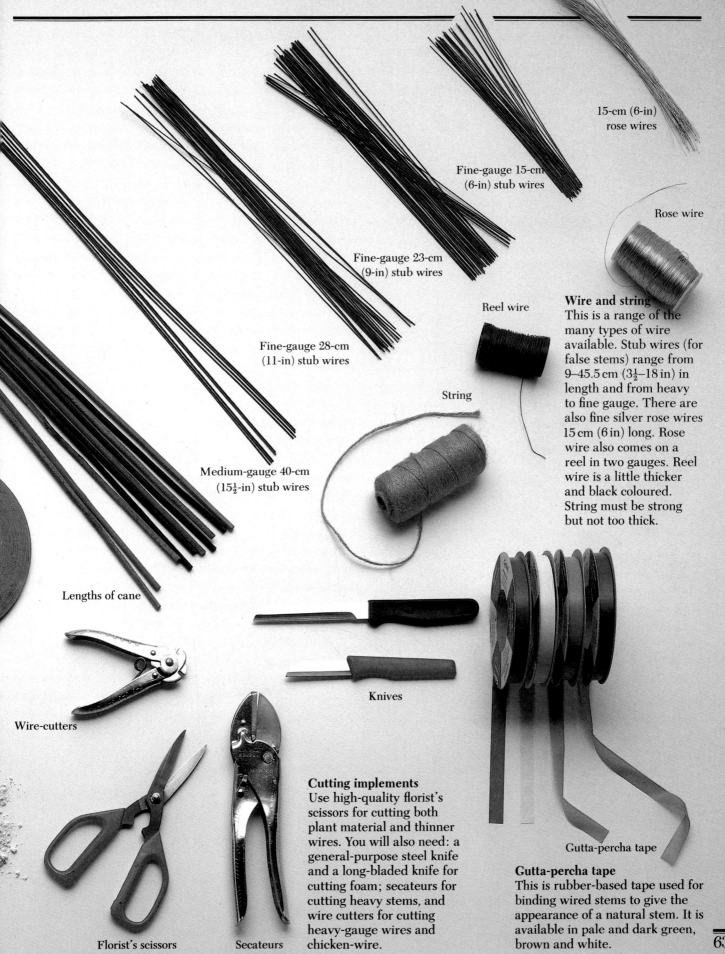

15-cm (6-in)
rose wires

Fine-gauge 15-cm
(6-in) stub wires

Fine-gauge 23-cm
(9-in) stub wires

Rose wire

Fine-gauge 28-cm
(11-in) stub wires

Reel wire

String

Wire and string
This is a range of the
many types of wire
available. Stub wires (for
false stems) range from
9–45.5 cm (3½–18 in) in
length and from heavy
to fine gauge. There are
also fine silver rose wires
15 cm (6 in) long. Rose
wire also comes on a
reel in two gauges. Reel
wire is a little thicker
and black coloured.
String must be strong
but not too thick.

Medium-gauge 40-cm
(15½-in) stub wires

Lengths of cane

Knives

Wire-cutters

Cutting implements
Use high-quality florist's
scissors for cutting both
plant material and thinner
wires. You will also need: a
general-purpose steel knife
and a long-bladed knife for
cutting foam; secateurs for
cutting heavy stems, and
wire cutters for cutting
heavy-gauge wires and
chicken-wire.

Gutta-percha tape

Gutta-percha tape
This is rubber-based tape used for
binding wired stems to give the
appearance of a natural stem. It is
available in pale and dark green,
brown and white.

Florist's scissors

Secateurs

63

WIRING

Flowers, leaves or other plant material often need to be wired to compensate for shortness or fragility of stem. Choose a stub wire from the range shown on pages 62–63 that will give adequate flexibility and strength as well as the length of stem required. Stub wire can also be used to extend short or broken stems. Gutta-percha tape is used to disguise the unsightly wire.

Wiring a flower-head

1 Almost all helichrysum flowers have weak stems. To wire a flower-head you will need a pair of florist's scissors, the required length of medium-gauge wire and a reel of fine rose wire in a cup to keep it from unravelling. Cut off the flower-head, leaving about 3.5 cm (1½ in) of stem.

2 Hold the stub wire against the stem so that it touches the base of the flower-head. Pull some rose wire from the spool and hold it about 5 cm (2 in) from the end.

3 Grip the rose wire in the same hand as the stub wire and stem, then, with your other hand, begin to wind the rose wire round.

4 Wind the rose wire tightly round the stem, stub wire, and loose end of the rose wire. Continue for 7.5 cm (3 in). Cut and fold in.

Everlasting flower
Helichrysum bracteatum

Mop-headed hydrangea
Hydrangea macrophylla

Holly oak
Dryandra quercifolia

Hybrid tea rose
Rosa 'Golden Times'

Hybrid tea rose
Rosa 'Sonia'

Everlasting flower
Helichrysum bracteatum

Love-lies-bleeding
Amaranthus sp.

Wild oat *Avena fatua*

Safflower
Carthamus sp.

Opium poppies
Papaver somniferum

Extending stems
You can extend hollow stems and make them flexible by inserting a stub wire into the stem itself.

Wild oat *Avena fatua*

Concealing the wire

5 Holding the wired flower upside-down, place the end of some gutta-percha tape behind the stem and at an angle of 45°.

6 Fold in the end corner of tape then twist the wire, keeping the tape taut so that it spirals up the wire and just overlaps itself. Continue just beyond the end of the wire, twist and break the tape to seal the end.

Wiring cones

1 Use heavy-gauge stub wire to form a stem for a cone. Push one end of the wire through the lowest band of scales so that 5 cm (2 in) juts out.

2 Wind the wire tightly into the cone. Twist the wire ends together to grip it.

3 Bend the twisted ends under the cone so that the long wire forms a stem from the centre of the base of the cone. Trim the shorter end neatly and conceal the whole length of the wire with gutta-percha tape, as described and illustrated on page 65.

Wiring bunches **1** Place a medium-gauge stub wire next to the stem ends, and, 5 cm (2 in) up, bend it behind the stems.

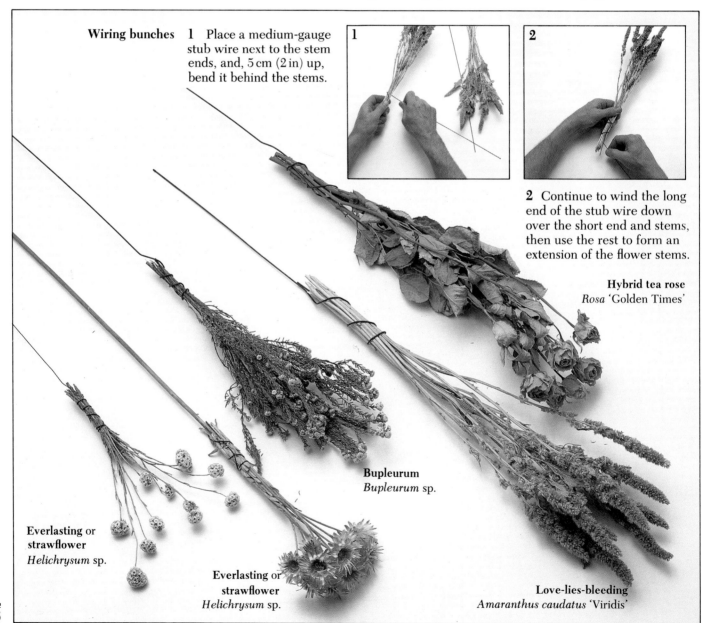

2 Continue to wind the long end of the stub wire down over the short end and stems, then use the rest to form an extension of the flower stems.

Hybrid tea rose
Rosa 'Golden Times'

Bupleurum
Bupleurum sp.

Everlasting or **strawflower**
Helichrysum sp.

Everlasting or **strawflower**
Helichrysum sp.

Love-lies-bleeding
Amaranthus caudatus 'Viridis'

Sugar pine *Pinus lambertiana*

Scots pine
Pinus sylvestris

Norway spruce
Picea abies

Larch
Larix sp.

Larch
Larix sp.

Monteray pine
Pinus radiata

Scots pine *Pinus sylvestris*

PREPARING CONTAINERS & BASES

Achieving a professional and satisfying result when arranging flowers involves good ground work. This includes preparing different types of container to the stage prior to adding the flowers, and making your own wreath and sphere bases if you want an alternative to shop-bought varieties. Time spent preparing saves arranging time later.

Preparing a basket

1 You will need some dry sphagnum moss, a sharp knife, narrow adhesive tape, medium-gauge stub wire and enough dry foam to overfill the basket. Use the base of the basket to indent a block of foam.

2 Using the indent mark as a guide, cut the block of foam to fit the bottom of the basket as tightly as possible.

Squat basket
Use dry foam and moss as below left.

Moss wreath base
This is a chicken-wire circle, filled with sphagnum moss (see p.73).

3 Top the block of foam with a second piece cut to form a mound 2·5 cm (1 in) above the rim of the basket. Then take the stub wire and loop one end to form an eye. Thread the adhesive tape through this eye and, using the wire as a needle, thread the tape through a cane on the inside of the rim.

4 Pull sufficient tape through to cross the basket with 15 cm (6 in) of tape to spare, then cut the tape and secure one end around the cane by sticking about 7·5 cm (3 in) of tape back on to itself.

Sphere
Cover a chicken-wire and dry foam ball with sphagnum moss (see p.70).

Saucer or plate
A shallow terracotta saucer is best mounded with dry foam and covered with silver lichen (see p.70).

Vine wreath
Entwined lengths of *Actinidia chinensis* vine can be used to make a wreath base (see pp.72–73).

Shallow dish
An open ceramic bowl requires dry foam and a covering of sphagnum moss (see p.70).

5 Pull the tape across the dry foam, pierce the rim again, and pull the tape tight, then unthread the "needle" and secure the tape. The dry foam may require further tape bands to hold it firmly in place if the basket you are preparing is large.

6 Cover the dry foam with a thin layer of dry sphagnum moss, ensuring that any gaps at the edges of the basket rim are filled. Notice how the unsightly dry foam is completely hidden in the prepared basket, top left.

Preparing a bowl

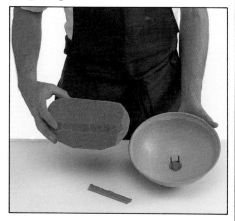

Shape a dry-foam block to fit the bowl and then impale it on a plastic prong, stuck in the bottom of the bowl with adhesive clay (see p.62).

Preparing a shallow saucer

Sculpt a mound of dry foam, if necessary using two blocks held firmly together with adhesive tape. Stick the foam to the saucer with strong glue to secure it.

Preparing a spherical vase

Stretch a loose ball of chicken-wire inside the vase until it grips the interior surfaces firmly.

Making a moss-covered ball

Moss-covered balls of various sizes are used for hanging and tree-type arrangements.

1 Cut a length of 30-cm (1-ft) wide chicken-wire, a little longer than the planned circumference of the ball. Make a mound of dry foam pieces on the wire, holding them in place with one hand while you lift an edge of the wire with the other.

2 Holding the first wire edge in place, lift and fold in the remaining edges gently, adding more pieces of dry foam to fill out the sphere shape as necessary. Mould the chicken-wire and foam to remove uneven or flat areas and turn sharp wire ends inwards.

3 Knot the end of a reel of reel wire (see p.63) to the mesh, leaving a long enough end for finishing off. Apply patches of moss and hold them in place, binding the wire around the sphere. The dark-coloured wire will not show against the moss, so use plenty to ensure that the moss is held securely.

4 When the whole sphere is covered with moss, bring the binding wire back to the long end of the starting knot and tie off, trimming the ends and concealing them within the moss.

Sculpting a small sphere
It is easy to sculpt dry foam to create whatever shape you require. Make a small sphere as follows.

1 Cut a cube from a block of dry foam, using a sharp knife. Pare off the corners of the cube with curving cuts.

2 Continue to pare away any edges, removing slivers of dry foam until you are left with a ball.

Preparing glass containers
The stems of dried material are generally unattractive and look particularly ugly seen through the sides of a glass vase. This problem can be overcome easily by lining the inside surface of the vase. To prepare the rectangular glass container, shown right, use adhesive clay to stick two shop-bought plastic prongs 12·5 cm (5 in) apart in the bottom of the container. Cut dry foam blocks to leave a 12-mm ($\frac{1}{2}$-in) gap between the foam and the container sides. Fix the dry foam on the prongs, then fill the gap with pot-pourri, using stub wires like chopsticks to ease the petals and flowers into place. The prepared container is the largest one shown below right.

Autumnal feel
Leave a 2·5-cm (1-in) gap between glass and foam to make room for golden leaves held in place by sphagnum moss.

Using lichen moss
(below centre)
If you use silver lichen moss to hide the foam, ensure the silvery ends of the moss are on display.

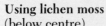

WREATH BASES

Shop-bought wreath bases are available, usually made from plastic and dry foam. However, you will find it more satisfying to make your own, following one of the methods shown below, and you will have full control of the size and style of the wreaths you make. Making wreath bases entails using damp or sappy plant material, which must be left to dry thoroughly before it is used with dried flowers, or your arrangement will quickly spoil. Drying can take up to a week, depending on drying conditions.

Making a simple moss base

1 Choose a commercially available wire frame and attach the end of a reel of string to it, leaving a short length beyond the knot. Take up a generous clump of damp sphagnum moss to begin covering the frame.

2 Place the moss on top of the frame and start to bind it firmly in place by winding the ball of string round and round the moss and frame. When bound-in, the moss should be approximately 2·5 cm (1 in) thick all round.

3 Feed in further clumps of moss, overlapping one clump with another and binding as you go. Be very careful to maintain the thickness of the moss as you continue.

4 When you reach the starting point, overlap with moss, and finish the binding. Find the original knot end, cut the string and tie it to the knot end to finish.

Making a stem circle
The stems of different climbing plants can be used to make wreath bases. The stems must be supple and cut into wands roughly 1.3 m (4½ ft) long. The stem circle, left, is made from actinidia vine stems.

1 Make a circle of the required size with one wand and secure it firmly with reel wire.

2 Take another wand, engage it near the binding, then twine it round the first ring.

Making a moss and chicken-wire base

1 Cut a piece of 30-cm (1-ft) chicken-wire to the length of the circumference of the base you want. Lay it flat, and arrange damp sphagnum moss along one edge.

2 Roll the wire tightly over the moss to form a solid tube approximately 3·5 cm (1½ in) thick; tuck in all the moss and turn in any sharp wires as you roll.

3 Bend the tube round evenly to form a circle, gradually curving it to keep the circle smooth. Do not overlap the ends; these will be sewn together neatly.

4 Attach reel wire to one end of the chicken-wire, leaving a loose end for finishing. Sew the two ends of the tube together, and tie and conceal the wire ends.

2

3 Continue to wind in the pieces of vine, allowing odd-shaped wands to form holes. Cut away the wire once the circle is self-supporting, and leave to dry.

SELECTING CONTAINERS

Most dried flower arrangements require a decorative container – a basket, a vase, a saucer, a dish, or some other receptacle. The choice of container is very important because, in a successful arrangement, container and plant material fuse to create a combined effect that is infinitely greater than that of either the flowers or the container separately. There should be a harmony of scale, shape, colour and texture between container and flowers. They should look completely natural together, as though they had always been meant for each other.

You will see in design guidelines on page 108 how every arrangement of flowers depends on its surroundings. The colours and textures of the walls and floors, the surface on which the arrangement is to stand, the space it will fill, whether it will be seen from all sides or from just one – these are all factors to be considered. With the location in mind, the arrangement can start either with the choice of container or the range of flowers that you want to use. Sometimes, because of a particular feature of its design – its textured surface, for instance, or its colour – it is the container that suggests the flowers. It is generally more difficult, however, to find a container to match a selection of flowers.

Strongly patterned or brilliantly coloured containers require either boldly simple or very dramatic arrangements, otherwise the container will dominate the flowers. Conversely, containers with simple shapes and plain colours lend themselves especially to arrangements with complicated colour combinations and unusual textures.

The range of container materials
The scope for choosing containers is enormous. They need not be expensive nor need they be watertight. In fact, your home is probably full of containers that you have never thought of as being suitable for dried flower arrangements.

It is a good idea to make a collection of containers to draw upon whenever you wish. Your collection should include containers in your favourite colours and ones that echo patterns and textures that appeal to you or relate to the decoration and furnishings in your home. Collect globes, cylinders, cubes and trumpets, classically proportioned containers or exciting contemporary shapes. They may be of basketwork, ceramic, wood, stone, metal or glass. They may be simple, mysterious or vibrant. Put aside any containers that appeal to you, whatever their shape or size, but bear in mind that it is easier to make arrangements in containers with necks that are a little smaller than their bodies.

A colourful basket
Unusually, the choice of flowers for this glorious summery arrangement preceded the painting of the basket. The colours of amaranthus, callistemon, achillea and hydrangeas, leucodendron cones and poppy seedheads, roses, larkspur and rhodanthe, silver helichrysum foliage and birch twigs are all echoed in the colouring of the basket. Spray paint and simple cardboard stencils were used for the irregular red and pink diagonal bands, which were then painted with smaller designs in silver, green and brown.

You should be able to find some glass containers in the kitchen – a tumbler, a jug or a bowl, for instance. And you may have a goldfish bowl or a small fish tank. If not, these can be bought relatively cheaply. All glass containers need to be lined with moss, petals or leaves, as the stems of dried flowers are not as attractive as those of their fresh counterparts (see p.71).

Wooden containers are particularly useful, as the wood itself combines strongly with the feel of dried flowers. From a wide variety of possibilities, you might choose a curved, olive-wood salad bowl or a small box decorated with inlaid wood. A rough wooden box that seedlings have been grown in can be used for an arrangement that imitates a mossy field or it can be filled with low, brilliantly coloured helichrysums, their heads peeping just above its rim. Take advantage of the worn colours of old painted wood or the jewel-like colours of lacquered wood from India or Japan to create some distinctive arrangements.

Baskets are also favoured for their natural qualities. You might consider a waste-paper basket, a shopping basket, an old needlework basket, a simple bread basket or, for a floor-standing arrangement, a heavy-weight log basket.

Try cake-tins and moulds, worn copper saucepans or iron casseroles, or, at the other end of the scale, perhaps an eighteenth-century silver jug or an oval pewter and brass Art Nouveau vase.

Search out ceramic containers with interesting glazes, such as lustrous metallic, pitted or crystalline. Raid the garden for terracotta pots, especially those with a mossy surface. Terracotta saucers can be transformed into marvellous dried flower gardens.

The garden is also the most likely source for stone containers such as urns and vases. They look splendid filled with enormous arrangements of dried flowers, the neutral colours of the stone complementing almost any colour combination of flowers and foliage.

Simple but dramatic (right) This dramatic dry-glazed turquoise vase demands simple treatment. A whirling white foam of gypsophila flowers complements its cool and slightly uneven surface and its trumpet shape. The flowers look as if they have been released suddenly after growing up from the bottom of the vase.

Decorated faience
An eighteenth-century French faience plate with beautiful painted decoration is the inspiration for this arrangement of dark, richly coloured roseheads nestling amongst their leaves. The sprinkling of bright blue cornflowers picks out the same flowers that are actually painted on the rim of the plate. The addition of a slightly brighter red rose seems to bring out the depth of colour in all the flowers.

Your own creations

Creating your own special containers can be extremely rewarding. You can do this quite simply by painting or covering an existing container. A light-coloured basket can be painted to complement the flowers you wish to use in the arrangement. Stencils can be cut from cardboard and a design created using spray paint. It is more effective if your colour shapes are large and bold: wide diagonal or vertical stripes make a good basic design. More colours can then be added in small areas to suggest texture or to echo the shapes of some of the flowers.

Alternatively, you might like to cover a basket or a simple kitchen bucket with a layer of plant material, such as moss, twigs or hay. Interesting effects can be achieved by mixing the moss or hay with some wild-looking flowers, such as helipterum daisies, heather, yarrow or cornflowers, especially if the flowers you choose will also feature in the arrangement. Either stick the mixture to the container with fast-drying glue, or roll the material around the container and tie with strands of raffia or ribbon. For step-by-step guidance to some of the many ways to create your own containers, see pages 84–85.

BASKETS & WOODEN CONTAINERS

There is a special affinity between both wood and wicker containers and dried flowers, since all the materials are the products of plants, cut and dried. Both types of container look natural and generally unobtrusive, so they mix with a wide range of plant material from exotic, brilliantly coloured flowers to the muted colours of foliage. You might give a basket a superficial sophistication by spray-painting it or by lacing strands of golden thread through its weave, and some wooden containers are painted and lacquered, but the basic materials always seem to retain their earthy vitality.

Baskets

Any plant that produces strong, flexible fibres can end up as a basket. Young willow stems (called osiers or withies) are most commonly used, and these range from the palest straw colour to rich russet browns, depending on how the bark of the willow is treated. Hazel and mountain ash stems are also used to make baskets, as are strips of oak, rushes, reeds and the leaves of exotic palms and bamboos. There are all kinds of decorative basket weaves and sometimes man-made materials, such as plastic and cardboard, are included to enhance the appearance of the basket and to strengthen it. Try to make the design of your arrangement complement the character of the basket by picking out a colour or colours found in the basket, or echoing the texture or shape, and incorporate the handle or lid if there is one.

Basket sizes range from pill-box size to pillar-box size, and this gives you great scope with dried flower arrangements. It is very expensive to fill larger baskets with dry foam as a basis for an arrangement. Instead, wedge the dry foam over a layer of broken polystyrene pieces (save it from packaging or ask at your local supermarket) or compressed newspaper.

Wood

Like baskets, wooden containers offset almost any groupings of dried flowers, foliage and seedheads. Old wood looks wonderful with an arrangement of dried flowers chosen to match the colours of old tapestry, and it is effective to match painted and lacquered wood with similar coloured plant material. You can use salad bowls, a cutlery tray, an old disused drawer or the many types of decorative wooden box that are sometimes inlaid or painted. In the garden shed you might find vegetable or plant trays, a garden trug and a cylindrical garden sieve, all of which can be the basis of charming arrangements. Junk shops or local auctions are also potential sources of interesting wooden containers of this sort.

Baskets
Any of these baskets could contain almost any mix of flowers. However, it is interesting to echo the colours of a basket in its arrangement, using flowers in light and airy colours and textures in the paler baskets and richer coloured materials in the dark ones. Basket handles can be made into a feature, lost in the arrangement, or even removed altogether.

Wooden containers
On the shelf, below, are containers as different as a wooden cutlery tray and a piece of hollow bark. The painted container was intended for waste-paper.

CERAMIC CONTAINERS

T hanks to the adaptability of clay, the choice of ceramics is vast and it spans many centuries. You can throw it on a wheel to produce round pots from thimble size to others more than a metre tall. You can cut it into slabs to make flat-sided vases or coil thin rolls of it to produce almost any shape, including giant pots a man could hide in. Many commercially available pots are moulded, so that they can be produced quickly in large quantities.

Glazes are made to produce an infinite variety of colours and surface textures and, although the more muted ones are safest for most dried arrangements, really bright-coloured vases like the trumpet vase on page 121 can make stunning containers. It is also useful to have some vases that match, perhaps with the same glaze or with exactly the same shape. These can then be arranged for several positions in the same room for a co-ordinated effect.

Types of ceramic
There are different types of ceramic, based on the sort of clay that is used and the temperature at which the glaze is fired in the kiln. Earthenware is fired at a relatively low temperature, is easily decorated and ends up with a very shiny surface. The majority of vases you see in shops are earthenware; but beware, dried flowers do not look at their best in shiny, ornately decorated pots of this kind, especially when the decoration is a naturalistic representation of flowers! Many ornate Victorian and Edwardian pots fall into this category.

Eighteenth- and early nineteenth-century earthenware containers have a very different quality. Time has worked to soften the look of the glaze (look at the bowl on page 119, for example). As pots of this period are quite valuable, place them where they will not be knocked. A table centre is a safe location.

The stony quality that pots fired to a high temperature possess (stoneware) gives their surface an appearance that is sympathetic to dried flowers even when they have a strongly coloured glaze. Porcelain is also fired to a high temperature, but this gives its surface a reflective, glass-like quality, although it is opaque. As with the shiny earthenware vases, it is better to use the less ornate porcelain containers for dried arrangements.

Try raiding the kitchen for a selection of simple ceramic containers. It does not matter if a bowl or jug is cracked, since it will not have to hold water and the crack can often be placed at the back of the arrangement where it won't be seen. Likely candidates are a casserole dish, a jug or mug, a sugar bowl or maybe a teapot, unused because of a broken lid.

Ceramic medley
This medley of ceramic containers includes, on the top shelf, a bonsai trough, a biscuit barrel, two matching stoneware pots and, at the end, a violently coloured slab pot. On the intermediate shelves to the right is an assortment of china and porcelain pots with an early tulip vase and Chinese bowl, and to the left, jugs and an umbrella stand. Below these is a group of stoneware and earthenware pots and mugs and, bottom right, a large stoneware cylinder with a smaller partner, a selection of vases and bowls, and a milk jug.

The less decorative a container, the bigger the variety of dried flowers you can use without the flowers clashing with the container. Since glass, metal and terracotta containers tend to be less decorative than ceramic ones, they open up a wider range of dried material for use.

Glass

Glass has a disadvantage for dried flower arrangers. If it is not completely opaque, it needs to be lined decoratively (with pot-pourri, moss, or perhaps coloured paper) so the dried plant stems are not on permanent show (see p.71). Simple rectangular, square or cylindrical clear glass containers are the easiest to use since they are visually undemanding. Coloured glass restricts the choice of flower colour and forces you to be more inventive. Most difficult to arrange in is sophisticated, highly reflective glass, which, like fine china and porcelain, can demand a formal arrangement.

Metal

The range of metal containers includes rustic, earthy objects made from iron, lead or weathered copper; utilitarian receptacles such as saucepans, casseroles, cake tins and moulds; and sophisticated items in the most precious of metals including goblets, tankards, plates and dishes, as well as vases and bowls. Pale pink flowers like roses and larkspur look beautiful in silver, while in gold (should you be lucky enough to have a gold vase or jug) try golden roses and delicate fern. Glowing, less sophisticated copper and brass look good combined with flowers in colours that themselves glow. Earthy metals will take almost any mixture of flowers as well as being the perfect foil for rich brown cones and twigs. Scour antique shops and market stalls for likely-looking metal containers. Old-fashioned metal scales, a copper kettle, or a Victorian soup tureen would all lend themselves to the creation of some unusual but effective dried flower arrangements; be bold in your choice!

Terracotta

Terracotta is red clay that has been fired in a kiln just once. It is usually left unglazed so is porous, but this matters not at all for dried flowers. The warm, matt outer surface adds life to all sorts of dried flowers. And the range of terracotta containers is immense, from tiny saucers, through strawberry pots and swagged urns, to giant olive oil jars made from coiled bands of clay. Even the simple flower pot can be elevated to a position in the sitting-room when arranged thoughtfully with dried flowers.

Glass containers
Glass containers range from cheap household items such as spaghetti jars, to the finest period vases. A period piece will itself suggest the style of arrangement to use. Look out for tiny, delicate glass containers – they have a quality you will find in no other material.

Metal containers
Every metal used to make a container has a character that can be enhanced by a flower arrangement – even rusted metal. Unusual boxes and tins can be effective, as well as the planters and troughs intended for pot plants.

Terracotta containers
Terracotta vessels are relatively cheap to buy and look particularly effective when filled with dried flowers. You might find an old storage jar or crock you can use in a junk shop.

ADAPTING CONTAINERS

Creating your own special containers allows you to make arrangements that are particularly your own. There are numerous ways to adapt household objects, such as waste-paper baskets and vegetable boxes, or you can decorate purpose-made containers to add a personal touch.

Completed hay basket
The finished hay basket is bound with three pieces of raffia and neatly trimmed.

Making a hay basket

1 Assemble a good-sized basket, (a bucket would also do), enough hay to give the basket a good thick covering, and some long strands of raffia to hold the hay in place.

2 Roll the basket in a layer of hay, using two long strands of raffia to keep the hay in place.

3 Tie the ends of the raffia tightly, adding further bonds if necessary. Trim and tidy the hay.

Decorated basket
An idea for adding to the decorative quality of a basket is to bind its handle and rim with some of the material that will be used in the arrangement. This basket has a handle covered with birch twigs bound-on with raffia. Raffia was also used to stitch twigs to the rim of the basket.

Moss-covered box
A wooden vegetable box makes an interesting container when decorated with a delicate mix of dried moss and flowers. In this example, little spikes of pink heather flowers and fluffy heads of alchemilla were mixed together with dry sphagnum moss. The outside faces of the box were spread with a moderately fast-drying glue and the mossy mixture pressed into place to cover the wood.

MAKING BOWS

What is more exciting than a beautifully wrapped present complete with bow and twirling ribbons? So it is with bunches of dried flowers either to give as presents or to have as decoration, hanging on the wall or placed on a shelf or windowsill. The bow does not need to be made with ribbon – many other fabrics and materials can be used to create a wide variety of different effects. The bow adds the finishing touch to the bunch, accentuating the colour combinations of the flowers and giving the bunch a particular style.

Making a simple bow

1 Leaving a length of ribbon for one end, make a figure-of-eight. Hold the ribbon with thumb and forefinger.

2 Leave a generous loop of ribbon, then make a second figure-of-eight on top of the first.

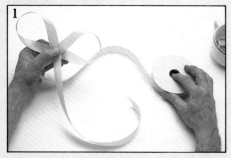

3 Pleat the centre of the loops to make them stand out. Bind and knot with reel wire.

4 Using the same ribbon, bind the stems of the bunch to cover any wiring. Tie the ribbon firmly.

5 Position the bow on top of the bound stems with the ends of the binding ribbon above and below.

6 Tie one bow in position with the binding ribbon. Cut all ribbon ends at an angle and tease the bow into shape.

86

Making a complex bow

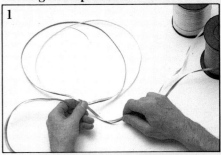

1 Make a ring about 25 cm (10 in) across with two string ribbons, keeping the ribbons the same length.

2 Make six more rings on top of the first, then take hold of opposite sides of the rings.

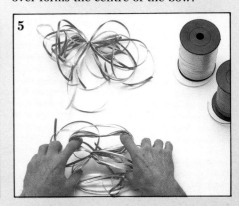

3 Bring the sides of the rings together to make a figure-of-eight. The cross-over forms the centre of the bow.

A plaited bow
A plaited raffia bow gives a simple country look. Make the plait first (see p.88), tying off each end to leave "horsetails", then make a figure-of-eight and bind it. Attach the bow to the bunch using raffia binding.

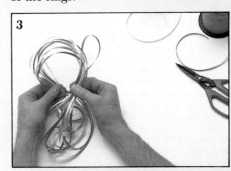

4 Tie the bow securely in the centre with another piece of string ribbon and cut the ends.

5 Tease the loops between your fingers and thumbs to open up and "loosen" the effect.

HANGING LOOPS

All hanging dried flower arrangements (such as wreaths, hanging bunches and swags) need to have a loop of some sort attached. Although loops are very often concealed from direct view, every detail on an arrangement you make is important. The loop you choose should complement your work so that, even from the back, the design is carefully considered. There is only one golden rule: use materials strong enough to support the hanging arrangement over a long period.

Making a loop for a wreath

1 Cover a stub wire with gutta-percha tape, twist a circle in its middle, and push into the back of the base.

2 Pull the two ends back under the frame, then push each end into the moss on each side to secure.

3 The loop hook appears in the middle of the back of the frame with its wire ends tucked in neatly.

Making a plaited loop
1 Attach a bunch of raffia strands, as thick as the required loop, to a firm support. Divide into three sections, and weave the left and right sections to the centre alternately, keeping the strands taut. Tie off the ends of the plait with more raffia and trim.

2 Form a plaited loop and bind the cross-over tightly using a stub wire, leaving ends that can be attached to a wreath.

Making a raffia loop
1 Take a streamer of raffia, and enclose it in the looped end of a stub wire before twisting the "eye" shut.

2 Using the stub wire like a needle, thread the raffia through the base. Pull the wire and raffia through and repeat in the opposite direction to leave a loop. Tie off the raffia and cut the wire free.

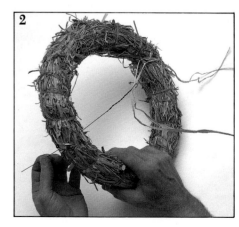

MAKING ARRANGEMENTS

W hen you have mastered the basic techniques, you can start to make arrangements. Although you can create an infinite variety of arrangements, there are some classic types that you will find in this section. They illustrate methods of construction that you will employ repeatedly as you gain in experience.

FAN SHAPE

One of the simplest kinds of flower arrangement is based on the shape of a fan. The lacy, one-sided example below, in a white lacquered basket, is a delicate mix of meadowsweet, pale-pink larkspur, deep-pink roses, white statice and green hydrangeas.

Making the arrangement

1 Create a fan-shaped back to the arrangement using some meadowsweet. The height should be approximately twice the height of the basket.

2 Now make a curve of meadowsweet, from the top centre to the front. Fill in the remaining meadowsweet to form a half-dome shape, so the stems appear to emanate from the centre.

3 Highlight the shape with spikes of pale-pink larkspur, roughly following the curves of the arrangement, then add heads of white statice, using the natural curves of the stems to accentuate the overall shape.

Light and airy effect
Pink roses are the next ingredient to be added, with some of their foliage left to strengthen the design. Lastly, fill in with wired florets of hydrangea, to make an airy arrangement.

POSIES & BOUQUETS

An attractive way of giving dried flowers is to make up a posy or bouquet. A posy is a compact and delicate all-round bunch of flowers, while a bouquet is usually larger and flat-backed. Combine colours and textures so that bunches can either be kept intact, or split up for use in other arrangements.

Informal posy
Here is the posy made in the step-by-step sequence, left, finished with a bow that both complements the arrangement and conceals the wiring (see p.86).

Making a posy

Summery bouquet
A mixture of green amaranthus, pink roses, silene, pink and white rhodanthe, yellow statice, bamboo and green hydrangea heads make up this brightly coloured summery bouquet, secured with a simple raffia bow.

1 Have ready a mixture of white larkspur, wired lilac-coloured hydrangea florets, campanula seedheads, quaking grass and pink statice. Begin by binding just two stems together using reel wire.

2 Add more flowers, binding them in one-by-one, to create a curved mound. Keep the flower-heads at differing heights for an informal country effect.

3 Towards completion add lower circles of flowers to cover the stems above the level of the wire.

4 Ensure that the flowers are well spaced before cutting and then tying the wire firmly.

Autumnal bouquet
This large fanned-out bouquet in autumnal hues is made up of nigella seedheads, exotic cones, pink and green grasses and seedheads of various colours. The whole is offset by a cream bow.

Feathery posy
The flowers in this posy have been chosen for their feathery qualities. Sweet-smelling lavender spikes and white helipterum flowers are combined with glycerined acacia leaves and deep-pink helipterum flowers.

Formal posy
This formal posy is composed of a circle of blue cornflowers, lilac-coloured hydrangeas, and tiny poppy seedheads surrounded by a ruff of lady's mantle. A blue string bow completes the simple effect.

93

HANGING BUNCHES

Both drying and dried flowers look marvellous hanging in bunches against a wall, from a beam, or even hanging on a cupboard door. When arranging a mixed bunch of dried flowers to hang on a wall, consider carefully both the scale of the bunch and the colours contained in it, just as you would a painting, to ensure that it suits its location, and becomes an integral part of its surroundings.

Wild bunch
This wild and imposing bunch includes green beech leaves, bamboo, intense blue delphinium flowers, and onion flower-heads. The bunch is attached to the wall by a length of plaited raffia (see p.88) with long strands of raffia trailing through the leaves and flowers.

Tying a mixed bunch

1 The flowers and grasses that make up this sunny bunch are cream helichrysum, alchemilla, white larkspur, *Helichrysum italicum*, phalaris, dill and green hydrangea. Bear in mind that the finished bunch will be seen from below, so look at it head-on as you prepare it. Arrange an initial bunch, using clumps of each of the longer stems in an informal way. Tie tightly with string well below the flower-heads. You can conceal the string with ribbon when all the ties are made.

2 Prepare a second, denser bunch to complement the first and then tie it to the first bunch, positioning the flower-heads a little lower.

3 Complete the bunch by tying in hydrangea heads at the bottom of the bunch and disguising the string ties with a bow (far right).

Textural bunch
It is the different textures of the flowers in this hanging bunch that make it so special. Clumps of white gypsophila accentuate groups of apricot-pink roses and spikes of *Limonium suworowii*. A few stems of green amaranthus and *Limonium caspia* are balanced by the group of pink hydrangeas.

Sunny bunch
This is the completed bunch, described in the sequence opposite. A lemon satin bow adds the finishing touch. Although each of these bunches looks effective alone, they also work well in combination.

HANGING SPHERE

Agreat glowing bunch, built up into a sphere of flowers and foliage can transform a stairwell or the corner of a room. For the most striking result, choose dried materials with strong variations in texture and colour and arrange them informally.

Making a hanging sphere

1

1 To create the stunning hanging sphere, right, you will need stub wires, a 3·5-cm (1½-in) curtain ring and red bottlebrush, pink helichrysum, pink and yellow roses, green amaranthus, two varieties of bupleurum, clumps of sea lavender and *Leucodendron meridianum*. These will be arranged boldly in clumps so that there are some larger areas of just one colour.

2

2 Hang the curtain ring at a convenient working height. Wire separate bunches of each ingredient (see p.66), leaving long wires for attaching. Wire the bunches to the ring one by one, leaving the stems short of the ring.

3

3 Wire in more and more bunches, bearing in mind where each will appear in the finished arrangement. The statice acts as the main filler while the spiky bottlebrush and the amaranthus serve to break the line of the curve.

The completed sphere
The last stage of making such a spectacular orb is to make minor re-arrangements of individual bunches and then to hoist it into its final position, from where the curtain ring at its top centre will never be seen.

WREATHS

We know from paintings and sculptures that wreaths (rigid circles of flowers and/or foliage) have been traditional wall or door decorations since early times, especially wreaths of sweet-smelling flowers, such as roses, and of aromatic herbs. There are various ways to make a wreath base, as shown on pages 72 and 73. The base you choose, whether it be wire covered in moss, plaited raffia or a knot of stems, will set the tone for the style of wreath you make. A wreath need not be packed with dried material around its entire circumference. If the base is itself decorative, you can allow it to show through, or leave a portion on display for a dynamic effect.

Making a small wreath
1 Take a dry, prepared moss base (see p.72). Wire sprigs of hops, flower-heads of ammobium, bunches of oats and single yellow roses. Cover the wired stems with gutta-percha tape (see pp.64–66).

A base of bound straw
This simple circle comprises pale-pink and cream helichrysum, cornflowers and gypsophila, all on a straw base. Generous pink ribbons provide the finishing touch.

Harvest wreath
The final effect of the wreath (made in the sequence above) suggests the mellow warmth of early autumn.

A whimsical wreath (right)
Entwined vine stems form the base of this wreath (see pp.72–73), decorated with rose leaves and pine cones. A nest of woven hay, complete with eggs, nestles in part of the vine weave, overlooked by a blue-bird.

2 Insert the stems of ammobium flowers into the base to provide the background to the wreath design, pushing each wire through the moss and bending it back into the base behind the wreath.

3 Decide where the hanging point of the wreath will be, then fill in the moss areas, offsetting clumps of the spiky oats and hops with roses and more ammobium.

Wild, natural feel (left)
Hay bunches, red roses, cornflowers, achillea and xeranthemum are bound informally with raffia.

A plaited-straw base
Plaited straw forms the ground for this wreath. A widening spray of blue and deep-pink larkspur, sweetly scented lavender, and delicate oats, falls in a semicircle, leaving part of the plait on view.

Incorporating ribbon
Pink ribbons, headed by a bow, are threaded and trailed through the vine stems of this wreath. Bunches of lilac-coloured hydrangea, peach roses and gypsophila are wired in between the woody stems.

Grass fan wreath
(below left)
A fan of grass stems, poppy seedheads and leucodendron cones partially covers the green sphagnum moss base of this wreath. Only the poppies and the cones required wiring.

FLOWER ROPES

The flower ropes that decorate this page are in reality nearly 1.8 m (6 ft) long, so they make striking hanging decorations on a grand scale. Once made, they can be used to festoon and garland, perhaps spiralling down the poles of a marquee or hanging either side of a fireplace.

Decorating a plaited rope

1 Plait and complete a very thick raffia rope (see p.88) to suit the length of your hanging space. Bind the ends firmly with raffia strands and trim neatly. Wire a small bunch of blue hydrangea flowers and brilliant yellow *Helichrysum italicum* (see p.66). Attach the bunch close to the beginning of the plait by pushing the stub wire into the thickness of the plait, and bending back the end to secure. Wire similar bunches to attach later.

2 Prepare plumes of blue tear ribbon by doubling a length, wiring it as shown, and then tearing down each ribbon-end. Insert the wire of a ribbon plume into the plait above the flower bunch, and bend back to secure. Improve the feathery quality by pulling each section of ribbon over the back of a knife to curl it.

The completed rope (left) In the finished rope the flowers and ribbons are arranged in groups at intervals down the plait. As finishing touches, some long, trailing ribbons were added towards the bottom of the plaited rope, and a raggedy raffia bow was made up and attached at the top to cover the securing tie.

Making an all-flower rope

1 Take red roses, pale pink larkspur and the delicate bamboo, *Arundinaria nitida*, and arrange a bunch in a loose fashion to suit the wild look of the bamboo leaves.

Using reel wire only, tie the bunch together securely at the top of the bunched stems. Cover the knot with a few turns of wire. Do not detach from the reel.

2 Holding the stems firmly, bind down their length and slip the reel through the last loop of binding before hitching it tight.

3 Arrange a second bunch and position it against the first so their flowers overlap. Bind the second bunch to the first and hitch tight.

The completed all-flower rope The rope can be as long as you like, depending on how many bunches you bind in.

SWAGS

A swag, or festoon, of dried flowers is a flower rope designed to loop from one point to another. A series of swags is known as swagging. It is usually prepared for a special occasion, such as a party during a festive season, a wedding or a christening. Long tables covered with crisp white linen cloths and heavy with delicious food look even more wonderful with complementary swagging making soft curves along their edges. Doorways, alcoves, shelves, banister rails, fireplaces, ceiling beams, all take on a new look when decorated with these flowery festoons, whatever type you choose to make.

Making a long swag is certainly time-consuming. However, one of the great advantages of using dried flowers is that they last, and can be arranged well in advance, so there need be no last-minute panic to finish before the first guests arrive. Equally, the swags will continue to look good long after the last guests have left.

Wire base swag
The completed swag looks very delicate in its pastel colours; it is, however, surprisingly strong. Cover the untidy end of a swag with a ribbon, or the beginning of another swag.

Making a swag on reel wire

1 One way of making a swag is to attach bunches of flowers to a wire. Flowers for this swag include hydrangea florets, roses, oats and gypsophila. First unroll sufficient reel wire for the length of swag required. Tie a loop at this point but leave the reel attached to allow you to bind the bunch later. Wire the hydrangea florets, and little bunches of gypsophila (see pp.64 and 66). Use them to make a posy, with the oats standing out a little at the top. Trim any over-long stems.

2 Place the bunch on the wire, directly on top of the loop, so that the flowers conceal it entirely. The loop will be used to hang one end of the swag when it is completed.

3 Holding the bunch stems against the wire with one hand, bind the bunch firmly, using the attached reel of wire. Pass the reel under the last loop of binding and pull tight.

4 Make a second bunch and hold it so that it overlaps the stems of the first bunch. Bind again with the reel wire and hitch. Continue in this way until the swag is completed.

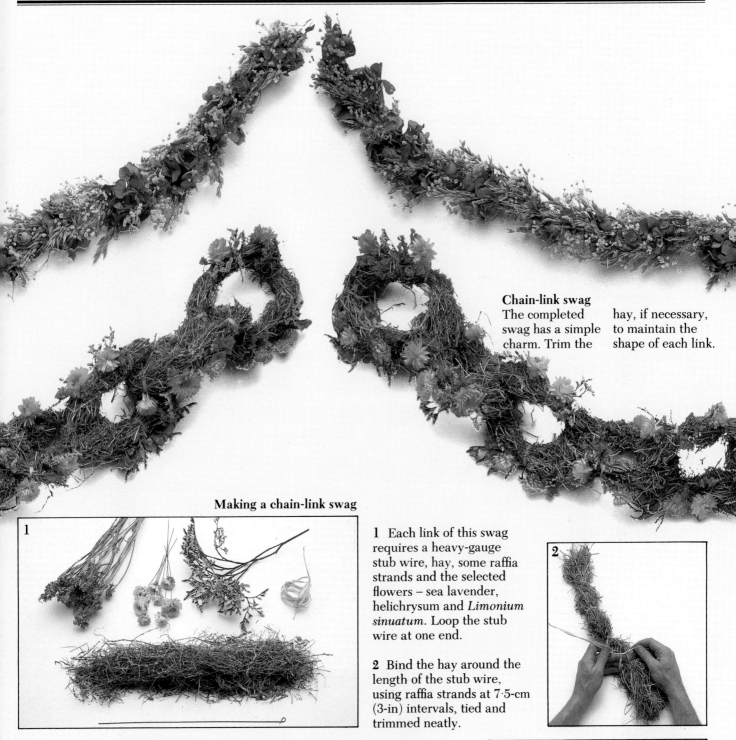

Chain-link swag
The completed swag has a simple charm. Trim the hay, if necessary, to maintain the shape of each link.

Making a chain-link swag

1 Each link of this swag requires a heavy-gauge stub wire, hay, some raffia strands and the selected flowers – sea lavender, helichrysum and *Limonium sinuatum*. Loop the stub wire at one end.

2 Bind the hay around the length of the stub wire, using raffia strands at 7·5-cm (3-in) intervals, tied and trimmed neatly.

3 Bend the bound wire into an oval shape, threading the end of the wire through its loop. Twist back the wire to secure the join and cover the link with another raffia tie. Tidy the ends to make the ring look continuous.

4 Decorate the ring with the flowers, tucking their stems under the raffia ties. Make as many individual links as necessary in a similar way. Finally, thread each oval through the preceding one to create the chain.

DRIED FLOWER TREES

A miniature "tree" made with dried flowers can look spectacularly architectural either as a free-standing floor arrangement or, on a smaller scale, like a Bonsai tree on a low table top. First, decide what height of tree you need, bearing in mind the objects that will surround it. Then use nature as a guide and look out for the shape of tree that would look good in your room. It could be based on an oak tree or a conical-shaped bay tree, a conifer or an open-branched magnolia. Find a piece of branch that will simulate the right sort of trunk and take great care to choose a complementary container.

Setting the trunk in an inner pot

Since the trunk must be firm and the tree base weighty, set the trunk in plaster-of-Paris in an inner pot.

1 Take some dry foam, plaster-of-Paris powder, a bowl and spoon, and a knife. Line a small clay pot with slivers of the dry foam. Plaster-of-Paris expands as it sets, and the pieces of dry foam will allow room for expansion and prevent the pot from cracking.

2 Mix the plaster-of-Paris powder to a thick, creamy consistency with the water. Two-thirds fill the pot with the mixture, making sure that the dry foam slivers stay in place. The plaster sets fast, so never reach this stage without having the trunk to hand! Also, keep some water handy to pour into the plaster-of-Paris mixing bowl as soon as you have scooped out as much as you need. This will prevent it from setting and cracking the bowl.

3 Insert the miniature trunk into the middle of the plaster – you will feel it reach the pot base. Wobble the trunk to ensure that the plaster settles and adheres all round. Supporting the trunk with one hand, turn the pot round slowly to see that it looks right from every direction, then spoon in more plaster to fill the pot to within 12 mm ($\frac{1}{2}$ in) of the rim. Support the trunk until it stands by itself. You can now begin making the head of the tree; either cone-shaped or mop-headed.

Making a cone-shaped tree

1 Impale a dry-foam cone (obtainable from florists) firmly on the trunk. Make staples by bending short, thin-gauge stub wires double, and use them to pin dry sphagnum moss to the cone.

2 Push dried flower stems into the dry foam through the moss, firstly using alchemilla as a background, followed by red roses and wired celosia, and finally fine twigs.

The completed tree
The final stages in making this tree, with its rich tapestry character, are to wedge the inner pot into an outer container, and to mound dried bun moss at the base of the trunk.

Assembling a mop-headed tree

1 Impale one lichen-covered sphere, a little smaller than the chosen container, on to the sharpened end of a curved and branched trunk, and a smaller sphere on a short branch lower down. The top, slim branch lends movement to the completed tree.

2 Take feathery ingredients, including meadowsweet, silver helichrysum foliage, poppy seedheads and green amaranthus. Arrange the ingredients in an informal way to make the head about twice the size of the container for the most striking effect.

The completed tree
The last stage is to complete the smaller head of flowers. A small branch is added to balance the higher branch and to harmonize all the elements visually.

DESIGN GUIDELINES

W hen you feel confident of your practical ability to make arrangements, it is time to judge your results and discover how to improve their aesthetic appeal. You will see in this section how, when designing your arrangements, you should consider the shape, texture and colour of both ingredients and container, and then how to relate these features to the location of the arrangement in your home.

The problem with making rules about the design of dried flower arrangements is that as soon as a rule is made it is possible to think of a beautiful and successful arrangement that breaks it. The arrangements on these two pages have been made to show how unwise it is to arrange according to rules. You might think that the flowers you choose dictate a certain type of arrangement but, below, the same plant material in three different containers has resulted in a range of beautiful displays. Conversely, if you

The same flowers in different containers (below) Three different containers – a trug, a small brass bowl and a short-stemmed glass goblet – have been used to create contrasting arrangements with silver-leaved mimosa. The different containers dictate both scale and mood.

feel that a container demands a specific arrangement, beware. Opposite, you will see three very different arrangements, all in identical containers.

Rather than trying to obey rules, the way to plan any arrangement is to consider the factors that will affect it once it is in position. Will it be standing on a table or a shelf or the floor? What size of arrangement would suit the location best? What colours, patterns and textures will surround it? From what angle will it be seen? Should it be an all-round arrangement or one-sided? By answering these questions you will begin to create an image in your mind of the arrangement you require. The result will be yours and yours alone, for no two people would ever create the same arrangement for a position in a room.

Nature as a guide

Nature can provide reliable inspiration for your arrangements. Plants usually have a way of growing into interesting and well-proportioned shapes and sizes. Stems and trunks are the right size to support the body of the plant and the size of leaves and flowers suits the scale of the plant. Studying natural forms will help you to avoid making arrangements that look as if they will topple over, or where the flowers look uncomfortably large for the container, or where the plant material looks too tightly packed.

The same containers with different flowers (right) These three arrangements employ identical grey fish-bowl vases. However, by creating three differently shaped and textured arrangements, the bowls themselves also appear different. Vibrant combinations would sit equally well in these subdued bowls. The arrangement, near right, is a simple, curved-topped, all-round arrangement using *Limonium caspia*, hydrangeas and amaranthus. In the arrangement, far right, (using straight pink grass stems, tall onion heads, spires of larkspur, eryngium and *Limonium caspia*) the stems have been left at their natural lengths – the flowers reaching out to three-and-a-half times the height of the vase. In the arrangement, middle right, leaves, cones and twigs curve down and out to the left to create a textured, fan-tail shape.

SHAPE

Dried plant material offers a vast range of shapes – some subtle, some dramatic. Leaves can be short and round, or long and narrow, wide and serrated, or delicate and fern-like. Flowers can be tiny, single with a few petals, or large and filled with intricately curved petals like an old-fashioned rose or a paeony. Seed-heads are infinitely varied and stems can be thin, curved, thick, straight, gnarled, contorted or thorny.

You can allow the various shapes of the plant material that you choose to dictate the shape of the arrangement. If you are using jagged leaves, for example, then make a jagged-shaped arrangement. Consider also the shapes of the spaces, and try to make these jagged, too.

A less naturalistic approach is to start off with a specific arrangement shape in mind and to build it – the cone-shaped tree, far right, is an example. Such arrangements require plant material that you can compact or build up, such as bun moss for mounding and sphagnum moss or lichen for carpeting.

Overall shape (right)
A conical tree is a simple shape to make (see pp.104–105). This one is covered with pink-dyed lichen, with a twirling rope of green hydrangea florets and small proteas as decoration.

Leaf shape
The differing shapes of these eucalyptus and acacia leaves dictated the shape of the whole arrangement placed in a pot-pourri-lined glass vase.

TEXTURE

The texture of an arrangement is a combination of the surface qualities of both the plant materials and the container you choose to put them in. Plant material abounds with texture. Leaves, flowers, mosses, grasses, seedheads and stems all have intriguing texture. It is not enough to produce a good strong shape in an arrangement; that shape has to be filled out with exciting textural variation. Spires and spikes against layers of leaves, soft groupings of petals in curves and curls, lines of interwoven twigs and areas of frothy flowers are just a few examples.

Learning from nature
A day in the country with a note pad will give you a wealth of ideas about texture. Take a look at a hedgerow with its complicated patterns of stems, twigs, leaves, flowers and seedheads. The manner in which plants interweave is full of extraordinary detail, revealed as the various surfaces catch the light. Look for designs on the ground among moss-covered stones, fallen leaves and seedheads, such as cones or beechnuts. Look at trees: the striated grain of their bark and the overlapping of branches as they disappear into the canopy of leaves. Notice the difference between large, densely packed leaves and those that are small and delicate and allow the light to filter through. Then there are the textural surfaces of the leaves themselves. Some fields are close-cropped, grassy curves of pastureland with the texture of velvet, while others have vertical lines of cereal stems, or soft, rippled surfaces of flowering plants such as brilliant yellow rape. This wealth of textures is inspiration for any dried flower arrangement.

Using textural plants
Leaves with special textures are particularly interesting as a foil for flowers. It is best to group them so that they overlap and cast shadows on each other. The delicate filigree structure of fern and acacia leaves are very useful for their mottled and veined surfaces.

Every dried flower has a textural quality of its own; the flat, rough-textured corymbs of yarrow, the beautifully arranged petals forming the cup of a paeony or rose, gypsophila with its white dotty froth, and the twinkling stars of open helichrysums. Such textures are a bonus to flower colour and should be mixed with care.

Adding seedheads to an arrangement will inevitably strengthen its textural appeal since the visual quality of most pods or other natural seed containers is largely textural. The range is wide, from the hard edges and points of conifer cones to the soft, fluffy heads of grasses.

Rustic arrangement
The countryside mix of plant material
in this arrangement was inspired by
the strongly textured, twig-covered
basket. The rustic quality of the basket,
with its uneven vertical binding of
twigs, is echoed by the arrangement of
hops, oats, poppy heads, hydrangeas
and pin oak foliage. Such is the
harmony between the textures of
ingredients and container that the
dried plants appear to be growing
out of the basket.

Light is made up of all the colours we see in a rainbow – the spectrum of white light, that is, red, orange, yellow, green, blue, indigo and violet. The colour of a flower that we see results from how much white light it absorbs and how much it reflects. Dried flowers are usually slightly muted in tone (the shade of a colour) compared with their fresh counterparts. Nevertheless, you will have seen in the ingredients chapter that the complete range of tones of colours provided by dried flowers is enormous. Among the

Single colour arrangement (left)
This cool, simple and elegant arrangement would look well against most coloured backgrounds, especially white or pastel ones. Blue, yellow or green backgrounds would give it extra strength, but red or purple would be uncomfortably dazzling.

Two-colour combination
The addition of achillea heads to the larkspur does not change the shape of the arrangement, left, but makes it warmer and adds a different texture. It would look good in an orange, yellow, white, blue or green room. In a pink room it would become vibrant.

primary colours (red, yellow and blue) there are many very good tones of reds and yellows, while blues are not quite so well represented. The range of tones from the secondary colours (those a painter can mix from the primary colours) is excellent. There are strong oranges, fresh greens and many rich purples.

Combining colours
Colours, and some of the tones of those colours, that lie close to each other in the rainbow mix with ease (see pp.116–117) and so it is generally safe to make arrangements using a combination of red and orange flowers, or orange and yellow, or yellow and green, green and blue, and blue and purple.

It is a little less safe to mix colours, and tones of those colours, that lie one apart from each other in the rainbow (see pp.118–119). These are mixtures of red and yellow, orange and green, yellow and blue, and green and purple.

The least safe combinations are of colours, and tones of those colours, that are two or three apart in the rainbow: red and green, orange and blue, yellow and purple. Describing a colour combination as less safe does not mean to say that you should not use it. Vibrant colour combinations can be very effective, as you will see on pages 120–121, but they are generally more difficult to locate.

Colour combinations also depend on the relative amounts of colours used. Again considering the most vibrant combinations, a very small amount of, say, bright red, in an essentially green arrangement will make the whole thing spring to life in the most extraordinary way.

As many dried flowers have soft, muted tones, it is easy to combine them in any way that suits your own colour demands or preferences. Do not be afraid of mixing any colours at all, or indeed using only one colour by itself for a bold effect.

Three-colour combination
A small amount of violet
larkspur added to the two-
colour combination, above
left, gives the arrangement
a new strength. Yellow and
violet become stronger in
each other's presence. The
three-colour combination
would look attractive
against white, yellow and
green backgrounds.

CLOSELY MATCHING COLOURS

It is simple to mix dried flowers with colours that lie close to each other in the rainbow. The combinations you see below and right illustrate that such combinations are not demanding, but neither are they boring. Each bunch is a collection of material that would arrange well in many different containers.

Pink and apricot (right)
A simple mixture in pink and apricot, using rhodanthe and pale terracotta cardoons.

Tones of blue (below)
This grouping of blues is made up of statice, deep blue larkspur and some sea holly.

Gold, yellow and green (below)
This group includes frothy alchemilla, wild achillea and green amaranthus.

Yellows and white (above)
This bunch is composed of yellow kangeroo paw, gypsophila and golden rod. The striking bright yellow globe flowers are of *Craspedia globosa*.

Rust, red and orange (above)
A bunch of red roses, rust helichrysum, red dahlias and orange carthamus.

Feathery summertime arrangement
A soft-coloured oval terracotta bowl was the inspiration for this arrangement. Its shape follows the outcurving sides of the bowl. Its ingredients appear in the bunch below.

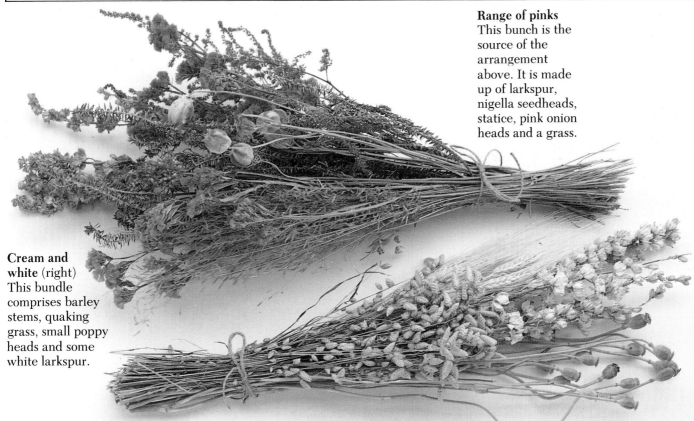

Range of pinks
This bunch is the source of the arrangement above. It is made up of larkspur, nigella seedheads, statice, pink onion heads and a grass.

Cream and white (right)
This bundle comprises barley stems, quaking grass, small poppy heads and some white larkspur.

117

CONTRASTING COLOURS

Flowers of colours that are next-door-but-one neighbours in the rainbow of hues, or of dissimilar tones of neighbouring colours, make harmonious partners, and their increased contrast has more interest than that of next-door-neighbour colours. However, this increased contrast makes it important to balance the volumes of different colours in an arrangement.

Blue and pink (right)
'Blue bee' delphiniums combine with bluey-pink achillea and echinops.

Cream, yellow and silver (below)
Silver *Stachys lanata* intensifies the yellow and creams of helichrysums.

Orange and yellow (below)
Chinese lanterns contrast with rich yellow yarrows and a froth of deep yellow alchemilla.

Pink and silver (below)
The strong pink of larkspur is offset by creamy-pink helichrysum and silvery acacia.

Terracotta, cream and green (right)
Terracotta-coloured rose blooms contrast with the green seedheads of chenopodium and the inflorescences of feather flower.

Cool, clear combination
This mixture of blue, straw-yellow and silver harmonizes beautifully with the early Delft flower-patterned bowl.

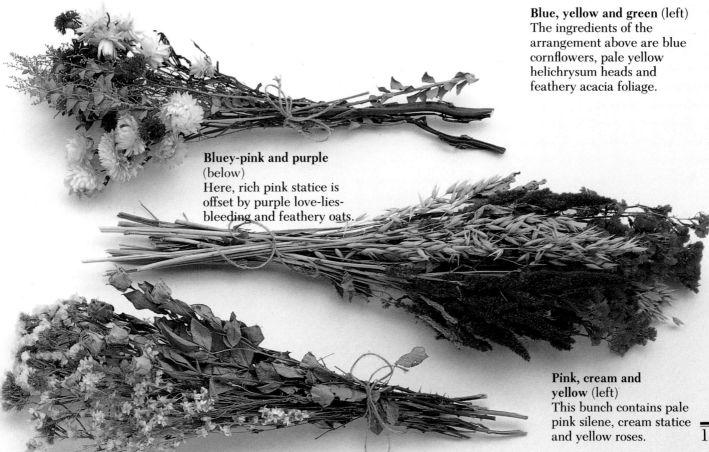

Blue, yellow and green (left)
The ingredients of the arrangement above are blue cornflowers, pale yellow helichrysum heads and feathery acacia foliage.

Bluey-pink and purple
(below)
Here, rich pink statice is offset by purple love-lies-bleeding and feathery oats.

Pink, cream and yellow (left)
This bunch contains pale pink silene, cream statice and yellow roses.

VIBRANT COLOUR COMBINATIONS

The bunches on these two pages show vibrant colour combinations that would make attractive arrangements. They either combine colours that are wide apart in the spectrum of colours, or tones that make strong contrasts despite their parent colours being close in the spectrum. It is easy for such strong groupings to fight with their surroundings visually.

Red and rust (left)
The red-pink, strawberry-like flowers of *Leptospermum* sp. in this bunch, with its silver foliage, contrast strongly with the rust colour of dock seedheads and *Limonium suworowii*.

Reds and greens (above)
This selection contains dark and bright red helichrysums, red roses, berried twigs with callistemon leaves, sycamore, amaranthus and lime-green solidago.

Lemon and scarlet (far left)
In this group, the contrast of bright lemon-yellow and scarlet is softened by the silver foliage of mimosa.

Orange and pink
It is the contrasting tones of bright orangey red and shocking pink rose blooms that make such a fiery combination above, especially against their green foliage.

Vibrant arrangement
The bold contrast of
scarlet, deep mauve and
green plant material in
this visually striking
arrangement is
perfectly suited to a
bright red casserole.

Scarlet, mauve and green
Scarlet bottlebrush and deep
mauve delphiniums make a
bold contrast together with
the cool, pale green of
hydrangea heads. These are
the ingredients of the
arrangement above.

There are many places in the home where dried flowers look attractive. The only positions to be avoided are those that bring the dried flowers into contact with too much moisture or humidity, or those where their colours will be bleached by direct sunlight. Despite these reservations, dried flowers will even last moderately well (perhaps six months or so) in kitchens and bathrooms as long as there is ventilation, especially if the arrangement consists of hanging bunches that cannot droop.

If the choice of locations in a home is wide, the choice of arrangement designs is wider still. But always let your design reflect the location of the arrangement. An arrangement that looks well on a side-table in the bedroom will certainly not look good when placed on the floor in the hall. The following pages offer advice on designing arrangements for particular locations.

Ceilings

The inspiration for decorating a ceiling with bunches of dried flowers is the beautiful sight of cut flowers hanging to dry. If the room or corridor ceiling you have in mind has good drying conditions (see p.170) you might indeed use fresh-cut bunches that will dry and become a permanent decoration. For drying purposes, however, fresh-cut bunches must be separate from one another to allow air to circulate between them, so you will not achieve the massed effect of the tight-packed dried bunches in the arrangement, right, while they are drying. The ceiling you use must be high enough to carry the dried flowers above head height. If it is too low, consider restricting the arrangement to a corner over a piece of furniture, such as a desk or side-table. If you intend decorating an entire ceiling, you can use garden wire strung between screw-eyes to support the bunches – the wire will be hidden by the final arrangement. Where the hanging will show, consider using bamboo or brass poles, iron pipes or even iron chains to hang the bunches from.

Covering a ceiling with flowers
If you want to decorate a whole ceiling, secure screw-eyes in opposite walls 15 cm (6in) from the ceiling, at 25-cm (10-in) intervals, and stretch strong, plastic-coated garden wire between each pair of opposing eyes. Arrange bunches of flowers and tie them 5 cm (2 in) or so from the ends of the stems.

To hang a bunch, part the stems equally and slip the garden wire into the cleft as right. The unsightly wires are gradually hidden by the overlapping masses of hanging bunches. A great mix of colours usually works well, but move the bunches around to vary the forms and the textures, as well as balancing the colours to achieve the best results.

Of all locations in the home for dried flower arrangements, the occasional table or low dining table is the most popular. An arrangement in such a location needs to be an all-round design since, even if it is not possible to walk around the display, its low position will always make the far side visible. A low-table arrangement requires, therefore, flowers that look good when viewed from above or from the sides. Roses, helipterums, achillea, statice and ammobium are just a few of the flowers that are ideal.

A good basic shape is a moderately low mound, which can be circular, oval, or even square or triangular if you wish. Once you have settled on the overall shape of the arrangement, the result will be more interesting if you use spires of flowers or foliage to break through the imaginary surface of the shape, and, conversely, create pockets of colour or texture below the surface, to give a layered effect.

Shallow containers suit the moulded shape of low-table arrangements best, keeping the overall shape from being too tall. Such containers have wide openings, so you will have to shape dry foam to fit inside the container as a medium to support the flower stems (see pp.68–71). Since you will be able to look down on the arrangement, cover the dry foam with a layer of moss before inserting the flowers, otherwise the unsightly foam will show between the stems.

When choosing your container and ingredients, consider colour and texture, as discussed on pages 112 to 121, but also try to include the colour and texture of the surface the arrangement will sit on, as well as the colour scheme and textures of the decoration of the room. You must decide whether your arrangement will blend or contrast with its location – whether it is to have a quiet charm or whether it will strike the eye immediately you walk in the room.

Proportions
The proportions of the arrangement must depend on the size of the table it sits on. You should never have to move an arrangement to make room for day-to-day activities. If it is the centrepiece of a dining table, for example, it must not interfere with comfortable eating, nor obscure the view across the table. On an occasional or coffee table, an arrangement must leave room for any other permanent objects, and space for a tray or a guest's drink.

Coffee-table arrangement
The success of this simple arrangement of white ammobium flowers depends on the linking honey colour of flower centres, plaited wooden container, and wooden table. The lid adds an interesting extension to the arrangement.

WALLS

anging an arrangement of flowers on the wall is as problematical as hanging a painting. The position of the container is crucial to the arrangement, since its height in relation to eye level dictates the placing and, to some extent, the type of flowers that you use. There is no point in placing an arrangement high on a wall if the flowers look best from above. So choose carefully. Your selection of plants might include helichrysum and statice (both of which have sideways-facing flowers), seedheads with good profiles (cereals and grasses) and those leaves that look good when viewed from most angles.

Several types of containers are made specially for fixing on walls. Choose from baskets, ceramic and terracotta half-bowls, and wooden and metal boxes. Remember that the container will probably be seen from an angle that reveals some of its underside and that, unlike a painting, an arrangement is three-dimensional and will probably be seen from both sides as well as from the front. Bear in mind that the direction of light falling on the arrangement will play an important part in the final effect. If you position them correctly, the container and flowers will interrupt light from the side and cast attractive shadows on the wall, adding another decorative dimension.

It is best to make the arrangement on a table or work top at comfortable working height. Offer it up to its wall regularly as you progress, to see how it looks when in place and to check on the various flower positions. Flowers and foliage can, of course, be wired so that they hang over the container. If you do this, however, make certain that they look natural, as though they grew like that. As with all arrangements, make sure that the flowers suit the container and aim for a simple and natural effect.

An informal arrangement
Orange-red helichrysum, golden barley and scattered bunches of hay look at their best hung just above eye level. The stems of pieces of corn were wired and bent over at a sharp angle so that they look broken. This, and the small group of yarrow heads, adds to the bold non-conformity of the rustic-looking arrangement.

Creating an arrangement in a container, purpose-made to hang like a three-dimensional picture, is not the only way of decorating walls with dried flowers. There is no reason why you should not hang beautiful, flat-backed bouquets of dried material directly on to a wall (see p.95) as long as you make a decorative feature of the tie – adding a bow or a raffia plait perhaps. A single bunch made with care, using ingredients that offset the decoration of a room, can be as effective as a painting. The downward-pointing flowers allow you to set the decoration high on a wall if necessary. You can use wreaths in a similar way for a more formal effect (see pp.98–99). Making groups of bunches or wreaths on a wall adds another dimension; they allow a larger scale of decoration and they can have a distinctly seasonal flavour.

Large-scale wall arrangements

If you have the space you can construct a complex wall hanging, such as the one shown right. This has the overlapping, massed effect of a ceiling full of hanging bunches, but flattened into two dimensions to give as much visual interest as a rare rug or a tapestry.

Against a white wall, the rich and varied colours and textures of dried flowers can be displayed delightfully. If you plan to make a wall arrangement against a coloured background, choose the ingredient colours carefully, not only to combine with each other, but also to suit the background colour.

Making a wall frame for hanging bunches
Fix hooks in the wall firmly, 1.5 m (5 ft) apart, to coincide with the top edge of the flower panel. Hang a length of chain from each of these so that you can slot 1.8 m (6 ft) bamboo poles through the links to form hanging rails. Compose your arrangement of bunches on the floor before tying them to the poles on the wall.

SIDE-TABLES & FLOORS

The similarity between these two locations is that they often demand large, imposing arrangements, usually made to stand against a wall, or a fire grate in summer. For this purpose they must have a fairly flat back and should be designed to be seen from three sides. If you have space, you might consider a floor-standing arrangement in the corner of a room, or even free-standing, away from walls or corners, when the arrangement takes on the same significance as a piece of furniture. These can be giant arrangements, reaching from floor to ceiling, or lower arrangements that cascade from a Versailles tub or a large basket.

Side-tables

A side-table is often a feature in a hallway, so any arrangement it supports is one of the first things to be seen on entering a house. For this reason it has great visual importance. Before starting the arrangement, study the relationship between the table, the wall behind and the ceiling above. The container and flowers you choose must suit the space between table and ceiling, as well as the scale of the table itself. The arrangement must also harmonize with any wall decorations nearby, such as paintings. The prominence of this kind of arrangement lends itself to bold shapes and intriguing textures and colours. Less dramatic arrangements are called for on side-tables in other rooms in the house, but the same principles of design apply when creating them.

Floors

A large, floor-standing arrangement is an imposing creation that requires a great deal of dried plant material. Some of the most effective are made in a simple way, using substantial branches and stems. For arrangements that reach towards the ceiling, you will need a large, weighty container that suits the natural forms of the dried material you choose. Such arrangements will be strong in shape and texture. Lower arrangements can include the more usual dried flowers as well as larger material.

Jug arrangement (far right)
A traditional jug filled with bulrushes is the perfect arrangement for a seventeenth-century side-table. The three varieties of bulrush tended to cluster vertically rather than spray out, so some dry foam was set in the base of the jug to hold the stems firm. The rushes now look good from the left, right and front.

Floor-standing arrangement (right)
This arrangement is simple, yet imposing. It stands 2 m (6 ft 6 in) high, from the floor to the top leaves, and comprises canes of feathery, silver-leaved bamboo and rust-coloured spires of wild dock seedheads that trace a delicate pattern above a rocky waterfall vase. It is a dramatic combination.

PEDESTALS

Pedestal arrangements are usually grand and designed to stand alone in a prominent position. Make sure that the pedestal is strong enough to support its load and choose a heavy container with a neck wide enough to hold a large number of stems. For very large arrangements dry foam can be piled high above the container's rim and bound with tape or enclosed in chicken-wire, so you can insert stems from low angles to reveal the full face of the flowers.

For best results, make the arrangement with the container already in position, by standing on a chair or step-ladder. Stand back from the arrangement at frequent intervals to ensure that the arrangement is well proportioned from every viewpoint.

Summery pastel arrangement
The flowers (many extended, see p.65) in this soft colour mix are: helipterum, kangaroo paw, gypsophila, wild bamboo, *Stachys lanata*, and fine grass and banksia foliage. The reconstituted stone urn contains a bucket with dry foam mounded to 20 cm (8 in) above its rim.

SEASONS & SPECIAL OCCASIONS

As your experience of making dried flower arrangements grows, you can look to events for inspiration, choosing ingredients and an arrangement style to suit the mood. This section shows dried flower decorations to celebrate the seasons, as well as others for parties and family occasions. The table and standing arrangements, bouquets, swags and garlands that are included can all be adapted to your own particular ideas and requirements. Let them act as a springboard for your own designs: they are there to encourage and inspire you.

SPRING

The first snowdrop of spring and the succession of flowering bulbs that follow are always a fresh delight – they are so delicate looking, yet so tough. Suddenly we realize with relief that the hours of daylight are lengthening, and at the same time we discover signs of new plant life, just a few scattered patches of tiny white flowers to begin with, but, as the sun reaches higher into the sky, the evidence of spring multiplies. Fresh green shoots appear in increasing numbers; then, before long, yellow daffodils are everywhere. Pale, but nevertheless, brilliant green and bright yellow are the predominant colours of spring: mossy banks and the edges of woods, parks and gardens come alive with narcissi. Here and there we glimpse a splash of blue scillas, or a touch of clear pink in the tiny alpine phlox.

Making the bank
To build a mossy bank on a large carving dish, stick florist's spikes across the plate (see p.62) and impale a thin layer of dry foam on them. Stick more spikes together in pairs, back-to-back, and insert one side of each pair of spikes into the foam, leaving the other side protruding, ready for pieces of bun moss. Decorate the bank with wired flowers.

The idea of representing spring with dried flowers might seem at first to be something of a paradox. Unfortunately, spring flowers themselves contain too much water to dry well. Bun moss, however, dries extremely well and, what is more, loses very little of its original colour in the process. And many yellow flowers lend themselves to drying. *Helichrysum italicum*, sparkling yellow statice and *Helichrysum bracteatum*, for example, all preserve a fresh spring-like yellow. With material such as this, you can create such an effective impression of spring that others will believe that your arrangement is created with fresh, and not dried, flowers.

A spring-like mossy bank
In the finished arrangement, groups of pink silene, stems of *Helichrysum italicum* and single blooms of bright blue delphinium, all wired (see p.64), have been inserted in groups through the moss. Tougher-stemmed achillea heads and white helipterum daisies complete an arrangement that looks as fresh as a spring day.

SUMMER

In a temperate climate, many of the short winter days are spent longing for the return of the colours and warmth that summer brings. At the beginning of the season, as the first roses begin to bloom, the grass turns a wonderful rich green, new fern fronds unfurl, and the first flower buds of summer-flowering shrubs, herbaceous plants and annuals begin to open – a foretaste of the rich mix of colours that fills garden borders in midsummer. The variety of summer's vibrant colours seems boundless: there are deep velvety reds and glorious pinks, brilliant yellows, sky blues, warm creams, deep purples, greens both acid and warm – all set off by spires, panicles and trumpets of the purest of whites.

The season's harvest for drying

This is the main time of the year to harvest for drying. At the start of the season, pick astilbe, early roses and alchemilla; a month later, yarrow, gypsophila, statice, helichrysum and ammobium. A little after, larkspur, rhodanthe and helipterum will be ready for picking; then, as the season draws to an end, hydrangeas and cardoons. Cut the flowers just a few days before they reach their prime and hang them in a cool, airy place to dry. Mature leaves and fern fronds can be pressed between paper under a rug or carpet (see pp. 176–177). Most summer-flowering plants dry easily and drying need not be done on a large scale. You might try hanging just a few bunches of garden flowers. These can either be used to make up arrangements or left in their drying bunches to provide a ceiling decoration for the kitchen, hall or living room, giving a taste of summer throughout the year.

Making up the basket

The mixture of flowers that is used to make up the summer basket, right, is divided by colour into four bunches, as above. Almost all the colours of the spectrum are represented. On the left, in the yellow, cream and white range, are *Helichrysum bracteatum*, gypsophila, yarrow, poppy heads and onopordum. In the centre are the glowing reds and pinks of roses, celosia, physalis, larkspur and helipterum; below, the blues of larkspur, echinops and lilac hydrangea. The green mix consists of pin oak leaves, fern fronds, amaranthus and hydrangea. The carefully spaced tiny heads of brilliant yellow helichrysum bring a liveliness to the arrangement.

Colours and textures of summer
The mix of flowers in this basket epitomizes the height of summer. Positioned in groups and singly, the flowers offset and complement each other in an arrangement crammed with rich colours and textures.

AUTUMN

The rich and bountiful array of summer flowers gives way to the traditional autumnal harvest as seedheads ripen and leaves turn to shades of rust and gold. Fields are full of rippling golden corn and the mellow sun casts long shadows as it circles lower in the sky. Early in the morning, dew lies in a haze over lawns, and in the evening the air becomes suddenly fresh and cool.

The season's harvest for drying
This is the time to harvest your own autumn leaves, flowers and seedheads. It is important to pick autumn leaves just as their best colours appear. Do not leave it too late! Once the sap begins to flow from them, they dry so quickly that if left a day or so too long, they will simply drop. You can either press the leaves individually or leave them on their stems and allow them to dry in a vase with a small amount of water left to evaporate (see p.170).

Many autumn flowers – small pom-pom dahlias, the feathery sprays of golden rod and the glowing orange lanterns of physalis can be hang-dried. Hydrangeas can be hung upside down and air-dried, too, or you can simply arrange them in a vase with a little water to dry by evaporation. Before picking hydrangeas, wait for the little flowers at the centre of each bract to wither. Seeding grasses, rushes, cereals and reeds should be picked at their prime. They are all easy to dry and can be either laid on paper or left standing in vases without water. Some seedheads, such as bulrushes and pampas, need to be set with spray (see p. 171) so that they do not break up as they would do normally to spread their seed. Bulrushes need a generous spraying to keep their heads perfectly intact, and should be dried as quickly as possible.

At this time of year it is wise to pick and start the drying process as soon as possible, before the wind wreaks havoc and the oncoming damp, cold weather causes the plants to rot.

Making the sheaf

Take a generous bunch of black-eared barley and, using three-quarters of it, make a central core of stems, building up layer on layer and binding each layer with string. Use the final quarter of stems to form an outer layer, securing it to the inner core with a single binding high up the stems so that they splay out in a spiral. Trim the stalk ends carefully and the central column will act as a pedestal. Add a plaited raffia circlet to cover the binding and decorate.

An autumnal combination
Rich golden leaves have
been arranged and dried in
a simple, trumpet-shaped
vase. The leaves fan out
almost to touch the barley
sheaf that stands alongside.
Although, in this case, the
two arrangements combine
to make a unified effect, they
could be separated to make
pleasing individual
autumnal arrangements.

WINTER

In winter time the landscape is populated by the skeletons of leafless trees and bushes, and the bare earth takes on a frozen greyness. The sun lacks warmth but, low in the sky, it filters between the bare branches and twigs. Only conifers and a few broad-leaved evergreens retain their leaves throughout the season, and the dark sombre green of those leaves seems to perpetuate the cold feeling of the landscape.

The season's harvest for drying
This is the season for collecting material that will provide both the structure and texture of many dried flower arrangements. All bare twigs and small branches dry well if cut in winter when the sap is low, and there is an infinite choice of shapes. Some twigs are covered with lichen, often delicate and intricately woven; others bear knotty cones that soften their stark lines. There are twisted vine stems, ideal for making woven wreaths while still damp (see pp.72–73) and, on the ground, you can find broken branches ideal for the "trunks" of dried flower trees. With plant leaves gone, many unexpected seedheads become visible: those of wild iris, clematis and hogweed, for example, together with the different cones that have dropped to the ground. Instructions for drying the damp materials you gather begin on page 170.

The most evocative winter arrangements of dried plant materials are sparse and gaunt-looking. Simple grey baskets can be filled with a multitude of different twigs, or with the branches of some conifer that does not drop its needles when dried – cedar and many types of pine and fir are suitable. Select branchlets with interesting shapes, and cut them cleanly with secateurs to avoid damaging the living tree.

Choose containers that have a cool appearance – opaque and shiny perhaps, like ice on a pond, or rough and grey-brown like frozen earth. You can match twig-covered baskets (see p.85) with skeletal arrangements of gnarled wood and bared seedheads. A narrow-necked vase can be the ideal container for a single conifer branch, especially one with several well-placed cones arranged on it.

Many sombre wintry effects can be transformed into festive arrangements by the addition of some brightly coloured material. Brilliant red and pink helichrysum heads, Chinese lanterns and the scarlet heads of bottlebrush all give a festive lift to the heavy green foliage and dark brown bark of winter. Twigs, together with seedheads and cones, can be given a seasonal sparkle by painting them gold or silver and then sprinkling them with shimmering gold or silver glitter. Hogweed and onion seedheads lend themselves well to such treatment.

Simple mid-winter arrangement
A few cone-bearing pine cuttings are a successful complement in colour and mood to this rust and bronze lustre vase. A broken web of fine-textured larch twigs bearing smaller cones provides the skeleton of this simple arrangement.

DINNER PARTY

A special dinner party to celebrate a birthday or anniversary calls for careful attention to decorative details that will help to make the occasion a memorable one. Using dried flowers in a creative way will lend a touch of magic to your celebration.

The dinner table itself is the place where your guests usually remain for the greater part of the evening. Once settled there, intentions to move to another room after eating are often forgotten in the relaxed after-dinner atmosphere. It is a good idea, therefore, to place your dried flower arrangements on the table and close to it, on a sideboard or side-table maybe. Alternatively, you could make a striking arrangement to hang on a wall in the dining room, or create an imposing floor-standing arrangement for a corner of the room.

The best dinner party arrangement ideas have a theme that usually starts with a single idea. It might be to limit the choice of flowers to a single bold colour through all the decorations, or to use a dramatic plant texture. In the arrangement, right, the original idea was to repeat the use of a novel container – a tiny ceramic "carrier-bag".

Guest's place decoration
Dainty ceramic carrier-bags contain a tuft of feathery pink, blue and yellow flowers set among spiky green foliage.

Overall harmony (right)
The colours and spiky shapes of the dried flower arrangements are similar in the tiny carrier-bags and the floor-standing Versailles tub.

Floor-standing arrangement (left)
Beside the table, but placed away from the chairs, is a white-painted wooden Versailles tub. It is filled with a mixture of tall pink, white and blue larkspur, enlivened by touches of brilliant yellow statice and feathery green foliage. This large arrangement is part of a repetitive scheme for decorating a dining room.

Table-centre arrangement (opposite)
Five miniature ceramic carrier-bags were filled with dry foam and a candle holder inserted into each, before being positioned in a radiating pattern. The same flowers and foliage that were used in the arrangements for each place setting were then built up to create a rough oval shape. It is important to flame-proof any dried plant material arranged together with candles, using a proprietary spray.

Alternative table centre
Another idea for a table centre mixes glowing red roses, clumps of silver lichen moss and pressed fern leaves, all arranged in a low, earthy-looking terracotta bowl. Place arrangements for each guest could be made with the same mixture of flowers in small terracotta flower pots.

HARVEST THANKSGIVING

Autumn comes and with it a sense of sadness at the loss of the long and easy summer days, but also a sense of something gained. As the crops are gathered in, as the evenings become colder, and fires crackle in the grate, this is the time to give thanks for all that nature supplies. It is an ideal time for a party, well before the spate of celebrations that occur at Christmas and the New Year.

It is also an ideal time for dried flowers. The bunches that were gathered in summer and early autumn are dry and ready to be used, and the autumn spectrum of colours – glowing golds, rusts and oranges – the colours of ripeness, are a joy to arrange. They can make you feel warm even when the weather outside is miserable. Think of the warmth of brightly coloured flowers like deep red pom-pom dahlias, golden rod, brilliant orange Chinese lanterns and the many colours of hydrangeas. Consider the ripened field cereals, sweet corn and wild grasses and seedheads of every conceivable kind. Shops and markets are full of fruits and vegetables that have the same glowing colours: rosy apples, golden pears, pumpkins, melons, squashes and gourds. There is no reason why you should not mix these with dried flowers in arrangements, maybe using a pumpkin or melon scooped out to form a container, or mixing fruits and dried material to make swags or to fill a basket. Use nature's abundant wealth to welcome your friends into the house with a glowing display in celebration of the year's harvest.

Shelf arrangement
Two flat-backed posies of autumn-coloured flowers threaded through single hydrangea heads are separated by a painted Welsh jug. The jug is simply arranged with bracken fronds, hang-dried dahlias and golden rod.

Welcoming hallway (right)
The swagging around the doorway frames a matching twisted-vine wreath on the door. A barley sheaf (see p.138) stands to the left of the door and on the right a two-tier table is decorated with autumn-coloured flower arrangements and a gourd.

Making harvest swags
(above and left)
Use a hay-filled roll of chicken-wire for the swag base, above (see p.73). Wire bunches of Chinese lanterns, barley and hay separately. Push heavy-gauge stub wire through the stem of each corn head, then wind around the stem to secure. Wire fresh apples through their cores, turn over the end of the emerging wire and pull it back into the core.

**Table-top
arrangement** (right)
A chubby golden gourd is neighbour to a figured mug filled with dried barley, grasses and many Chinese lanterns, and a spilling hay-covered cornucopia.

CHRISTMAS

A welcoming holly and pine wreath on the front door; a blazing log fire in a hearth, richly swagged above with pine branches and cones, and bright red and pink flowers and ribbons; garlanded pictures; red, green, silver and pink arrangements of foliage, flowers, nuts, cones and ribbons – these are just a few of the images evoked by Christmas.

Use roses, helichrysum, callistemon and Chinese lanterns to make wonderful vibrant garlands, wreaths and arrangements that echo the festive mood of this long season. The wintry-looking foliage of many pine species is ideal for both fresh and dried arrangements. Spray-paint twigs and leaves in silver and gold, sprinkling on glitter dust before the paint dries. Wire nuts and cones (see p.67) and either spray them silver, red or gold and cover them in glitter, or simply varnish them if they are to be mixed with brightly coloured flowers. Holly, unfortunately, does not dry, so if you include it in your Christmas decorations you may need to replace it before the season is over.

Try making Christmas tree decorations from dried flowers. Stick together groups of four or five bright-coloured helichrysum heads to form small spheres and hang them on the tree beside the more traditional glass and paper decorations. Little posies of multi-coloured dried flowers also look very attractive.

Tea caddy arrangement
The twigs and eucalyptus leaves, above, were sprayed with silver paint and glitter dust for a festive look.

A wealth of arrangements
A Christmas tree, decorated pictures, fireplace, table-top and wall arrangements add up to a warm festive scene.

150

Festive wreath (left) Three branches of blue pine, each 60 cm (2 ft) long, and some silver-coned twigs were tied together to form the basis of this wreath. Red, pink and silver ribbons cascade from a silver bow, which covers the tie. To complete the wreath, the branches were decorated with clusters of red and pink helichrysum heads and some pink spheres and ribbons.

Dramatic swagging (above) The asymmetric swagging over the hearth is balanced visually by a festive picture. Two swags were made, each by overlapping a series of bunches (see p.100).

Ingredients include: dried pine branches, red and pink helichrysum heads, twigs with silver-glittered cones, the strawberry-like heads of leptospermum, and fresh, variegated holly.

Simple flower-pot arrangement (above) A chicken-wire sphere (see p.70) was covered with dyed-green lichen and dotted with bright red berries on wires.

Natural-looking arrangement (right) The spiky twigs rising from a froth of sea lavender, and eucalyptus leaves give this arrangement an airy and informal appearance.

Informal basket (left)
This arrangement comprises a dark green, lichen-covered basket crammed with pieces of blue pine foliage and glittering silvered walnuts and cones, together with twinkling sprigs of feathery gypsophila dusted with glitter and a scattering of bright red berries.

Formal wreath (below)
Four green candles are set in a formal combination of clematis seedheads, deep pink roses, pale pink helichrysum, green hydrangeas, green lichen and spikes of agonis and osmunda fern. This elegant arrangement has a mossed chicken-wire base (see p.73).

This day, one of the most important in many people's lives, is always associated with flowers. The bride and her bridesmaids always carry flowers and often have flowers entwined in their hair. The church and reception area are bedecked with flowers and traditionally the bride and her groom are showered with flower petals. Fresh flower bouquets look wonderful on the day, but sadly they soon wilt and die. Dried flowers can be kept for many years as a keep sake of such a special day.

Another great advantage with dried flowers is that you can make bouquets, head-dresses, swagging and any other decorations in your own time, if necessary several weeks in advance of the wedding date.

Colour theme

It is important to establish a colour theme for the flower decorations for a wedding. This does not mean that the same flowers need to be used in all the arrangements, just that the colours and general textures should match. Although an all white wedding is undoubtedly very beautiful, it is now more usual to use a mixture of white and other cream or pastel coloured flowers, or completely multicoloured mixes.

Bouquets and posies

The bride's bouquet can be made to many different designs. The most important factor is to make sure that the flowers are easy to hold and that the bouquet is proportioned so that it looks important but not overpowering. Nowadays, bouquets are rarely longer than 45 cm (18 in), shaped like a tear drop and varying in style between very formal and very wild. Some brides prefer to carry a posy, the flower decoration most favoured for bridesmaids (see pp.92–93), and there is also the option of carrying a beautiful bunch of flowers cradled in the arm.

Dried flowers at the reception

Buffet tables and the table for the wedding cake can be decorated with swags (see pp.102–103), with matching bows attached to the points of the swags. The cake can be edged with flower-heads and topped with a small vase of matching flowers. Arrangements can also be prepared for pedestals and table tops (see pp.132 and 124).

Ready for the celebrations
Swags of flowers have been tacked to the edge of the wedding cake table. The cake is decorated with flower-heads below and a tiny arrangement on top. Beside the cake is the bride's bouquet and on the chair, in front of the pedestal, are the bride's head-dress and bridesmaid's posy.

Making the bride's head-dress

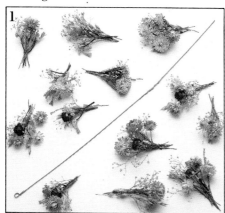

1 Make small bunches of ingredients. Join two stub wires, twisting an "eye" in one end and trimming the other to 5 cm (2 in) longer than head circumference (measure with string). Cover with gutta-percha tape.

2 Bind on the bunches using reel wire, covering each binding with gutta-percha tape. Conceal the "eye" with the first bunch and cover the stems of each bunch with the flowers of the next. Leave 2.5 cm (1 in) of stub wire.

3 Bend the decorated stub wire into a circle and thread the 2.5 cm (1 in) of free wire through the "eye", and bend back to secure. The flowers of the first bunch on the stub wire should cover the stems of the last bunch.

Completed head-dress and bouquet (below)
The completed head-dress, made in the sequence left, is shown below, next to the bride's bouquet. When the head-dress is placed on the bride's head, its flower bunches can be teased into position. The bride's bouquet is a simple bunch bouquet (see p.92) made with flowers to match the head-dress, including bright pink roses, gypsophila, pale creamy pink helichrysum, yellow kangaroo paw, oats and some feathery foliage. Use the longest stems first and make sure that all the thorns are removed from the rose stems.

Cake top arrangement
A small silver jug is ideal for carrying a posy of flowers for the top of the cake. As well as roses and helichrysum to match the bride's bouquet, this little arrangement includes some spiky white leptospermum, leucodendron stems and fluffy silver foliage.

Bridesmaids' flowers (right)
Here are three types of dried flower arrangements for bridesmaids to carry. The little basket of flowers is perfect for a very young bridesmaid; it is small, light and easy to hold. The pretty little sphere of flowers is favoured by 5–10-year-olds and is based on a moss-covered ball of dry foam. A posy can be carried by a bridesmaid of any age. The stems can be bound with ribbon, starting near the flower-heads (see p.158).

Making a spray bouquet

1 Wire and cover every stem of the ingredients, then make a flat-backed spray, three-quarters the length of the bouquet, binding each flower and leaf in with reel wire. Trim and cover with gutta-percha tape.

2 Continue to bind in ingredients, gradually fanning out the shape, until they "trail" to a sufficient length. Bend the bound wire stems as you go to form the handle by which the bride will hold the bouquet.

3 Bind in further stems to form a posy shape above the trailing spray. Wired stems make it very easy to move each flower or leaf. Cut and tie the reel wire and cut the stem of the bouquet to 17.5 cm (7 in).

4 Make a trailing ribbon bow and, using the same ribbon, bind down the handle, leaving an end for tying.

5 Bind to the end of the handle and back. Tie the two ribbon ends with a simple under and over knot and use the ends to tie on the bow.

6 Although this style of bouquet is formal, the outline is kept irregular.

FLOWER IDEAS

Dried flower decorations can be other than arrangements of stems in containers. Many of the ideas in this section are ideal for gifts, and include using dried flowers for their scent as well as their appearance, making pictures with pressed flowers to mount and frame, and creating exquisite miniature arrangements in a wide variety of containers.

POT-POURRI

Rose petals, lavender, mimosa, pinks, lilies, jasmine, violets, honeysuckle, paeonies and orange blossom all retain their perfume for a long time after drying. While a mixture of these scented flowers alone will emit a delicate fragrance, a more pervasive perfume is achieved by adding herbs, spices, seeds, bark, oils and fixatives, to make pot-pourri.

There are two methods of making pot-pourri. The original method uses partly damp material and gave rise to the term pot-pourri, which means "rotten pot". You layer partly dried petals of scented flowers with salt and store in a sealed container for about two weeks. Then you mix in herbs, spices and a fixative and store in a sealed container for a further six weeks. Finally, you add fragrant oils or essences in very small quantities and store for another two weeks before placing in a pierced, lidded container. The second method uses wholly dried material and is more popular nowadays. You mix dried, fragrant petals with dried herbs, spices, fixatives and oils and store in a sealed container for six weeks. Then place the scented mixture in open bowls.

RECIPES

Fresh, green scented mix (dry)
1 cup each: lemon-scented geranium leaves, lemon verbena leaves, mimosa flowers, myrtle leaves
¼ cup orris powder
Grated peel 2 lemons
4 drops each: citronella, rose geranium oil
Decoration: ferns & helichrysum flowers

Cottage garden mix (moist)
5 cups scented pink rose petals
2 cups each: marigolds, paeony petals
1 cup each: bergamot flowers, honeysuckle flowers, scented pinks
4 cups natural salt
½ cup allspice
⅓ cup orris powder
6 drops each: rose oil, rose geranium oil, bergamot oil

Lavender mix (dry)
3 cups lavender flowers
2 cups pale pink rose leaves
Grated peel 2 lemons
1 cup each: lemon balm leaves, leptospermum leaves, sweet woodruff
¼ cup orris powder
4 drops lavender oil

Spicy mix (moist)
1 cup each: juniper berries, bay berries, myrtle cones, sandalwood cones, Jerusalem

thorn, rose hips, bergamot flowers, rose petals
2 tbsp each: ground cinnamon, cloves
½ cup each: sliced ginger root, pounded allspice, anise seeds, red lichen, patchouli
Grated peel 3 oranges & 3 limes

Fragrant garden mix (moist)
2 cups each: pale pink rose petals, lime blossoms, white lilac flowers
1 cup each: philadelphus flowers, lily of the valley flowers, lippia leaves, chamomile flowers, white dianthus flowers, myrtle leaves, rose geranium leaves
4 cups sea salt
6 drops verbena oil
4 drops lily of the valley oil
30 g (1 oz) gum benzoin

Rose mix (dry)
8 cups dried red rose petals
1 tbsp ground cloves
2 tbsp each: ground allspice, cinnamon, orris
4 drops rose oil

Woody mix (dry)
4 cups cedar twigs
2 cups cedar bark shavings
1 cup sandalwood shavings
2 tbsp orris powder
4 drops each: cedarwood oil, sandalwood oil
Decoration: cedar cones, pine

Cottage garden mix

Fresh, green scented mix

Lavender
mix

Spicy
mix

Fragrant garden mix

Rose mix

Woody mix

FRAMED FLOWERS

Many flowers and leaves retain much of their colour and delicacy when pressed, and it is well worth pressing all sorts of flowers, grasses and foliage. Narcissus, scillas, primroses and snowdrops all look very attractive when pressed; so, too, do daisy-shaped flowers and the smaller stems of heucera, forget-me-not, gypsophila and crocosmia. Fleshy, succulent plants do not usually press very successfully, and very full-petalled flowers, such as roses and paeonies, look ugly when pressed because their flower-heads are too bulky and their petals overlap and fold. Sometimes, however, overlapping petals can create attractive patterns, particularly those of trumpet-shaped flowers such as lilies and tulips.

The most attractive way of presenting pressed flowers is to make a two-dimensional arrangement and mount and frame it. There are no hard and fast rules for designing pressed flower pictures. Be guided by the nature of the material itself, recalling the way that it grows and the grouping of its flowers and foliage on the plant. Samplers and botanical paintings may also provide inspiration for your designs. Position flowers and leaves on a sheet of good quality, matt monochromatic card – off-white or cream is usually

Arranging pressed material (above)
The pressed leaves being positioned, above, will create the finished picture below. The simple arrangement is given elegant form by pointing all the stems in the same direction towards the base of the card.

"Sampler" (opposite)
A border of rose leaves frames groups of violas, lace-cap hydrangeas, cow parsley and an anemone.

Simple arrangement (below)
The mixture of colours and textures provides interest in the foliage picture, below.

best. Try using different combinations of flowers and leaves. Why not use some smaller leaves or flowers to make a border? Rose and fern leaves make particularly effective borders, so, too, do the silver leaves of *Cineraria maritima*, and trails of small-leaved ivy can work well. Be careful not to position flowers or leaves too close to the edge of the card or they may be obscured by the frame – broad margins are safest. When you are satisfied with your design, simply lift and stick each piece of material in position. Use either a latex-based adhesive, placing a tiny spot on the centre of the back of the flower or leaf, or a clear plastic adhesive spray. If you do use a spray glue, though, you will need to make sure that the material is positioned correctly first time, as, once in position, it is difficult to remove the material without damaging it. Choose a simple frame that does not detract from the delicacy of the flowers and leaves.

GIFTS

Not only do dried flowers make very special presents as arrangements, they also lend themselves well to decorating and perfuming other gifts. A single rose and a fern frond, or a simple tiny posy of lavender and mimosa attached to the bow on a parcel adds a beautiful finishing touch, and the lavender will also emit a delicate fragrance.

Pot-pourri and pomanders

Pot-pourri (see p.160) can be used in a wide variety of presents. Fill cotton or linen sachets for placing in drawers and wardrobes, or stuff cushions or pillows with pot-pourri. Make sure, though, that the perfume is not too strong if filling a pillow. You might like to place pot-pourri in a hand-crafted ceramic bowl. Try to complement the colours of the bowl with the pot-pourri and, after wrapping it in clear film, add a matching bow. Pot-pourri can also be sprinkled over the mossed foam base of a dried flower arrangement to add colour and perfume to the arrangement.

Pomanders can be made from citrus fruits. Cover an orange, lemon or lime with cloves, leaving a space about half the size of a clove head between each one, so that when the fruit has dried and contracted, the cloves will cover the fruit completely. The point of a clove will pierce the skin of oranges fairly easily, but you may need to pierce limes and lemons with a needle first. Leave a gap all the way round the middle of the fruit, so that you can attach a ribbon afterwards. Sprinkle the covered fruit all over with powdered orris root – ground nutmeg and cinnamon can also be added – and wrap in a paper bag and store in a cool, dry cupboard until it is completely dry. Alternatively, fill metal or ceramic spheres with pot-pourri, or place spices and orris or patchouli leaves in a lidded basket.

Scented candles and pressed flowers

Scented candles are easy to make and you can buy candle moulding and dipping kits from craft shops. Traditionally, *Myrica cerifera* (wax myrtle) is added to the wax to perfume it. Other myrica species produce very sweetly scented berries with a waxy surface that can be separated from the berries by boiling. Alternatively, you can add flower or wood oils to the wax. To make a moulded candle that is both attractive and sweet-scented, line the mould with pressed flowers and leaves before pouring in the wax.

Pressed flowers can also be mounted on to thick paper to make cards and pictures (see p.162). Use a latex-based adhesive for sticking the flowers to the card and place only a very small amount of glue on the material to prevent the delicate flowers and leaves from being damaged.

Parcel with lavender and mimosa sprigs

Sleep pillow filled with hops

Glass jar layered with pot-pourri

Scented and decorated candles

Clear plastic box of pot-pourri decorated with pressed violet petals in clear film

Sweet-scented dried flower
arrangement

Ceramic bowl of
pot-pourri

Pressed flower and
leaf gift cards

Orange pomander

Parcel with rose and
fern decoration

Bag of pot-pourri

Wardrobe or drawer sachets
and pot-pourri

Raffia spice basket

MINIATURES

Dried flowers lend themselves extremely well to miniature arrangements. Their jewel-like quality is highlighted by the small scale. A large flower or seedhead from a protea, artichoke or thistle, or a fir cone, can look attractive on its own in a small container, but arrangements composed of groups of either mixed or the same variety of flowers are generally most effective. Try arranging a few stems of wheat with some strawflowers, or some cornflowers with little daisies, in moss in a small, low basket or in a tiny jug or vase. You can stand such an arrangement on a bedside table, for example, or you can make a grouping of miniature displays on a shelf or side-table. The scope for creativity is enormous: how about making a miniature garden on a small, moss-covered plate, or setting flower-heads amongst pebbles on a little dish? These are intricate to make, but great fun, and well worthwhile when you see the finished result.

A muted arrangement
This tiny basket makes a good foil for the brighter mixtures on these pages. Leucodendron cones nestle on a mossed base between green phalaris seedheads.

Baskets within baskets
Several miniature baskets can be filled with brightly coloured flowers and either used singly or combined, as above, in a larger basket. Two miniature baskets are fitted into a basket tray: one holds a mass of blue larkspur heads embedded in sphagnum-moss-covered dry foam, while the other is filled with a mixture of bright orange statice and light green oats.

Red roses in hay
Bright red 'Mercedes' roses are set in hay-covered dry foam. Hay is bunched up between the roses and the occasional field grass seedhead added.

Pink roses with silver
Set on a mossed base, the
intense pink of 'Mullard
Jubilee' roses contrasts with
the bright silver of
helichrysum foliage.

Red, green and silver
The strawberry-like flowers
of *Leptospermum* sp. are
interspersed between rose
leaves, set through moss into
a foam base.

A bright, three-colour mix
This little basket contains
eryngium heads and blue
cornflowers set on a bed of
pink helipterum daisies.

Three baskets in one
A basket of tiny pink
clustered everlasting on a
mossy base sits beside one
filled with ammobium and
gypsophila. Across one end
of the basket tray is a violent
mix of purple statice and
yellow helichrysum heads.

167

Roses with oats
A tiny silver jug holds 'Gerda' roses with a few leaves and green oats to offset them.

Artichoke head
The glazed onion-shaped vase would seem too small to hold an artichoke head, yet the combination looks just right.

All silver
A single silver carline thistle combines with a group of stachys flower-heads to striking effect in this silver mug.

Exotic combination
A Sheffield-plated tea caddy holds *Craspedia globosa* flowers and yellow kangaroo paw. The copper colour of the caddy makes a vibrant combination with the golden flowers.

Lemon helichrysum
A minute silver bowl is crammed with helichrysum.

Pink helichrysum
Bright pink helichrysum flowers spill out from the deep blue glass liner of a salt cellar – simple, yet so effective.

A lustre vase
This hexagonal lustre vase contains a simple bunch of striking miniature poppy seedheads and gypsophila.

DRYING
&
OTHER SKILLS

The following pages contain the practical details of drying methods for fresh flowers and other plant material. They also show how to repair damaged specimens, effect modifications, such as skeletonizing leaves and changing the shape and colour of flower-heads, and how to store plant material once it is dry. Also included in this section is a selection guide to help you choose the most appropriate plant material for your dried flower arrangements.

AIR DRYING

Air drying is the simplest and most commonly used of the four basic methods of preserving plant material. All you need is a dry, cool (no less than 10°C, 50°F) room with circulating air. The best locations for air drying are a cool airing cupboard, a spare room, an attic or loft, a garage or a shed.

Depending on the form of the plant material, you can dry it lying flat, upright in a vase or simply hanging in bunches – the method used for the majority of flowers (see p.173). Make sure that air can circulate around the flowers, leaves and seedheads easily. Leaves especially hold a lot of moisture and if several stems are packed closely together the leaves are likely to rot before they dry.

Drying flat

Most grasses, bamboos, fungi and twigs dry well when laid flat. Leaves shrivel when dried in this way but keep their colour well and retain their natural shape on the stem, which is not the case if they are dried upright or hang dried. Lay the material on an absorbent surface: cardboard, newspaper or even wooden floorboards make excellent drying bases. A linoleum, tile or stone surface will need to be well covered with card or paper. Space the plant material out carefully so that air can circulate around the stems and leaves.

SUITABLE PLANTS

Drying flat
- Lavender
- Bamboo
- Dock
- All grasses
- Giant hogweed

Drying upright
- Acanthus
- Eucalyptus
- Sea lavender
- Chenopodium
- Mimosa
- Hybrid delphiniums
- Gypsophila
- Hydrangea

Drying in boxes
- Sphagnum moss
- Bun moss
- Lichen
- Selaginella

Supported by a wire rack
- Globe artichoke
- Sweet corn
- Onion seedheads
- Carline thistle
- Protea
- Lotus seedheads

Drying upright in a vase
There are two methods of air drying plant material upright. Tall grasses and seedheads, such as pampas, dock, bulrushes, onion seedheads, sea lavender, *Limonium sinuatum* and chenopodium, dry well when left standing in an empty vase (right). Flowers such as hydrangeas, mimosa, hybrid delphiniums, gypsophila and lachenalia dry better when stood in about 5 cm (2 in) of water. The stems first absorb some of the water, which gradually evaporates, leaving the plant material to dry out completely.

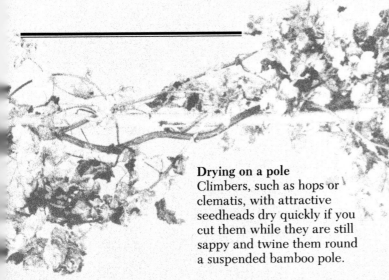

Drying on a pole
Climbers, such as hops or clematis, with attractive seedheads dry quickly if you cut them while they are still sappy and twine them round a suspended bamboo pole.

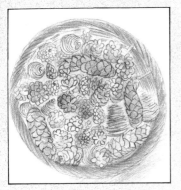

Cones in a basket
Cones begin drying while still on the tree. Collect shapely cones from the floor of woods or pick them from garden trees and simply lay them in a basket or on a plate for a few days at room temperature until there is no moisture apparent between the scales.

Heavy-headed flowers
Large flower-heads are best dried individually, supported by a wire rack. Secure chicken-wire horizontally and slot each flower stem through the mesh. The wire must be supported high enough to allow long stems to hang freely. This method of drying is excellent for globe artichoke heads, large protea flowers and sweet corn. Leave the husks of sweet corn in place during the drying process.

Moss in a box
All mosses are easy to dry. Simply lay the moss in a single layer on a bed of crumpled newspaper in a box or on a tray. Do not pack the moss tightly or it will rot. One of the most attractive mosses when dried is bun moss, which grows in bright green hummocks. Silver lichen is also beautiful and sphagnum moss, which dries to a beige green, is ideal for use as a base (see p.69).

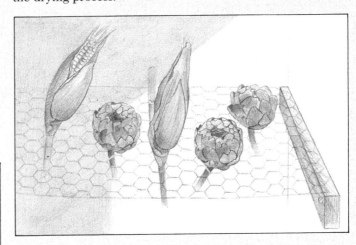

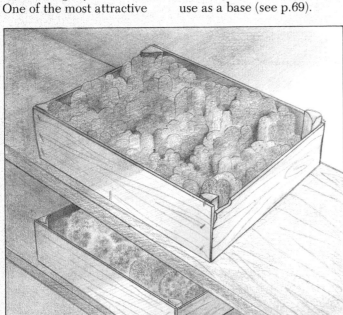

Spraying grasses and rushes
The seedheads of some grasses, especially pampas grass and bulrushes, break up during drying if their surface is not sealed. Pick such grasses before they reach maturity and spray them liberally with hair lacquer or another fixative. Make sure you spray them well or they will quickly disintegrate while drying.

Wiring for hanging – first method

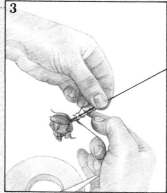

1 Fresh flowers with very short stems, (for example, multiflora roses), should be wired before drying. Take a medium-gauge stub wire and hold it firmly against the stem. Use thin reel wire to start the binding, as for dried flowers (see p.64).

2 Wind the reel wire down the stem, binding the stem and stub wire together firmly. Continue winding down the stub wire beyond the fresh flower stem. Cut off the reel wire when you reach the bottom of the stub wire to secure.

3 As when wiring a dried flower-head, cover the extended stem with gutta-percha tape, starting just beneath the fresh flower-head. Keep the tape taut and revolve the wired stem until it is completely covered with the tape.

Wiring for hanging – second method

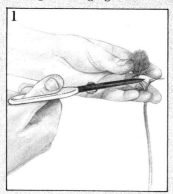

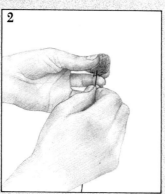

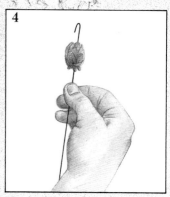

1 Some flowers, particularly helichrysums, are best wired by another method. Hold the flower bud gently with one hand and cut the stem just below (always use buds that are about to open).

2 Take a medium-gauge stub wire and insert it into the underside of the flower bud in the centre. The wire should enter the bud at the same point as the stem originally began.

3 Push the wire through the base of the flower-head and up through the flower centre so that it protrudes about 5 cm (2 in). Take care not to damage the petals as you ease the wire through.

4 Bend over the stub wire 2.5 cm (1 in) from the top. Pull the wire back through the flower so that the open end of the "U" pierces the base of the flower. Squeeze the "U" round to secure.

Bunching wired stems

1 Flowers wired when fresh to prevent their heads from flopping over are very easy to hang dry. Bunch together about 10 flower-heads and bind with an elastic band.

2 Gently bend the stem wires so that none of the flower-heads touch, allowing air to circulate between them. Finally, hang them upside-down to dry.

SUITABLE PLANTS

- Roses
- *Helichrysum bracteatum*
- Larkspur
- Statice
- Yarrow
- Helipterum
- Rhodanthe
- Chinese lantern
- Golden rod
- Mimosa
- Bottlebrush

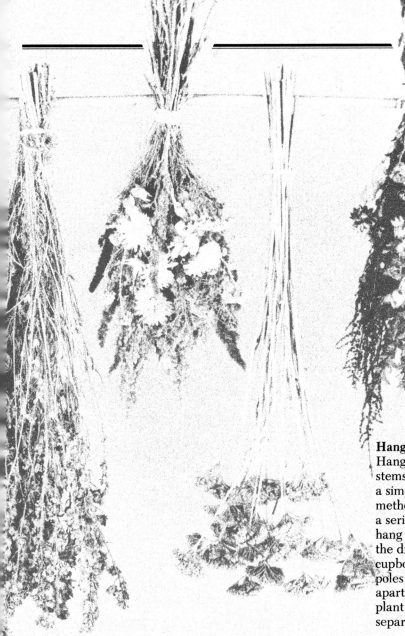

Hanging

Hanging bunches of plant stems upside-down to dry is a simple and very useful method of air drying. Set up a series of poles or wires to hang the bunches from in the drying area – a linen cupboard is ideal. Space the poles about 25 cm (10 in) apart to ensure that the plant material is well separated. Fix the poles or wire at least 15 cm (6 in) below the ceiling to allow enough room for the stem ends. Either hook the bunches over the poles or attach them to the supports with string or raffia ties.

Bunching fresh-cut stems

1 Make sure that the stems to be air-dried are good specimens, and not likely to break when hung. Pick them just as the flowers (such as the rose above) approach full bloom, no later.

2 Remove the lower leaves and any thorns from the stems and cut away any damaged material to leave bare stems where the bunch will be tied as trapped leaves will cause rot.

3 Assemble a bunch of about five flowers, staggering the positions of the flower-heads. Tie the bare lower stems together loosely with string or raffia. Spread out the flowers so that the heads and leaves are well separated and the air can circulate freely around them while they dry. If they are too close together, petals and leaves are likely to rot.

GLYCERINE

A few flowers, such as hydrangeas, moluccella and heathers, can be preserved using glycerine, but the best results are achieved with leaves. The advantage of using glycerine to preserve plant material is that the material remains supple. The disadvantage is that leaves and flowers change colour quite substantially when preserved in this way, usually becoming khaki or fawny-brown. The plant material is placed in a mixture of glycerine and water. As it absorbs the mixture, the water content gradually evaporates, leaving the material saturated with glycerine.

Prepare plant material by removing the lower leaves on the stems and cutting the base of the stems at a sharp angle so they take up the mixture well. Hardwood stems should also be split and hammered. Stand the material in water for a couple of hours to recover and start taking up water. Make the glycerine solution with 40 per cent glycerine and 60 per cent very hot water, and stand the plant stems in a container with 7.5–10 cm (3–4 in) of the mixture at the bottom. For softwood stems make sure that the vase supports the material well. Keep the material in a cool, dark place while it is absorbing the glycerine. The time taken for the process to be completed varies according to the density of the plant material but begin checking its progress after about six days.

SUITABLE PLANTS

- Copper beech
- Eucalyptus leaves
- Pin oak leaves
- Laurel
- Elaeagnus
- Hydrangea
- Moluccella
- Ivy
- Magnolia leaves
- Aspidistra leaves
- Choisya leaves
- Mahonia leaves
- *Senecio greyi*
- *Phlomis fruticosa*

Preserving leaves

1 Immerse large individual leaves or sprigs in 50 per cent glycerine and 50 per cent water until the colour changes completely.

2 Remove them from the solution, wash in a mild detergent and lay flat on newspaper to dry.

Leaves preserved in glycerine will remain pliable and retain their individual characteristics.

Preserving stems

   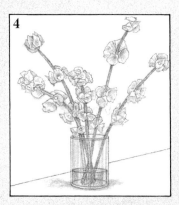

1 Remove leaves and any bracts from plants such as moluccella (above) from the bottom 10 cm (4 in) of stems.

2 Bunch the moluccella stems together and cut the ends of the stems at a sharp upward angle.

3 Place the stems in a container and pour in about 7.5 cm (3 in) of the glycerine-and-water mixture.

4 Place in a dark, cool place for about 10 days, but check for complete colour change after a week.

DESSICANTS

Dessicants (or drying agents) such as silica gel, borax, sand, or a mixture of all three can be used to absorb the water content from flowers and leaves. Plant material dried in this way looks very like its fresh original in form and colour.

Silica gel drying
Silica gel dries plant material quickly and the crystals can be used over and over again. It is available from chemists in two forms: as white crystals and as crystals with a colour indicator. Colour-indicator crystals are bright blue when dry and turn pink when they have absorbed moisture. The crystals must be ground down in a mortar and pestle to at least half their original size before use so they envelope efficiently.

Place a layer of dry crystals, approximately 1.2 cm ($\frac{1}{2}$ in) thick, in a container (such as a biscuit tin or jar) that can be sealed. Lay wired heads of flowers or

leaves on top, then add more crystals, brushing them between the flower petals with a paintbrush and covering the flowers or leaves completely. Close the container, making sure it is well sealed. Check the material after two days: it should be firm to the touch and colour-indicator crystals should have changed colour. Remove the material from the container as soon as it is dry, otherwise it will become brittle. To re-use the crystals simply heat them in a shallow tray in a warm oven; store them in an airtight container.

Borax, alum and silver sand drying
Borax and alum are powders and benefit from being mixed with fine dry silver sand before use: mix three parts chemical to two parts sand. Follow the procedure for silica gel drying but wait at least 10 days before checking to see if the material is dry. To re-use the mixture dry it out in a low-heat oven.

Drying in a biscuit tin

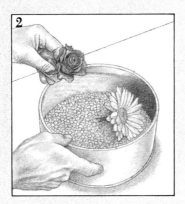

1 Pour 1.2 cm ($\frac{1}{2}$ in) of fine-ground, bright blue silica gel crystals into the base of a biscuit tin that has a tight-fitting lid. The crystals must be completely dry.

2 Place the flower-heads, already wired or with short stalks, on the bed of crystals, positioning them so that they can be covered completely with the crystals.

3 Ease the crystals between the petals of the flowers with a spoon or brush and then push them over the petals so that the crystals hold the flower in a natural position.

4 As soon as you have covered the flowers, put the biscuit tin lid in place and stick adhesive tape around the edges to seal it. Store in a dry place.

SUITABLE PLANTS

● Roses	● Lily flower-heads
● Paeony	● Narcissus
● Zinnia	● Larkspur
● Delphinium	● Ranunculus
● Dahlia (small varieties)	● Anemone
● Freesia	● Gerbera
● Gentian	● Camellia
● Hellebore	● Orchid

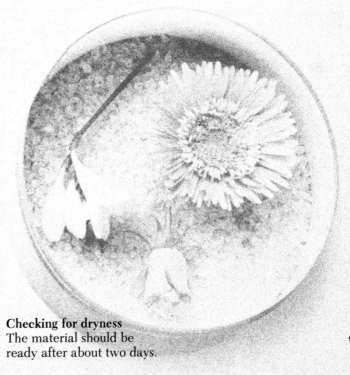

Checking for dryness
The material should be ready after about two days.

PRESSING

A simple method of drying plant material is to press it. The result is two-dimensional but natural colour is retained extremely well. A home-made or bought flower press give the best results, although a heavy book or books can be used or plant material can simply be placed under the carpet.

To make a flower press you will need two heavy wooden boards, preferably of hardwood, although thick plywood can be used. Drill coinciding holes in the corners of both boards to accept four bolts with securing wing nuts. Alternatively, you can bind the press together with straps or thick nylon string. Place the flowers or leaves to be pressed between two layers of blotting, or other absorbent paper, and position layers of thick cardboard either side of the blotting paper. The card prevents the shape of one layer of material from being imprinted on the adjacent layer of plant material.

Cut the plant material you wish to press on a dry day and place it in the press immediately. It is best to avoid plants that have fleshy leaves, such as sedums and other succulents, or very three-dimensional flowers, such as larger orchids, as the shape would be extremely distorted by pressing. The stamens of flowers tend to stand out from the centre of the flower and can be either gently flattened with the fingers or allowed to stand up while the surrounding petals are pressed flat. For the latter, cut a hole the size of the stamen cluster in the blotting paper, and also in the cardboard spacer (you can use a slice of dry foam for large flower centres), to allow only the stamen to sit upright in the press (see opposite). The length of time plant material takes to dry depends on the density of the flowers or foliage, but check it after about 10 days.

SUITABLE PLANTS

- Pansy
- Lace-cap hydrangea
- Lily
- Freesia
- Anemone
- Hellebore
- Nicotiana
- Ferns and most foliage
- Hosta
- Marguerite
- Primula
- Snowdrop
- *Polygonum affine*
- Clematis

Traditional press

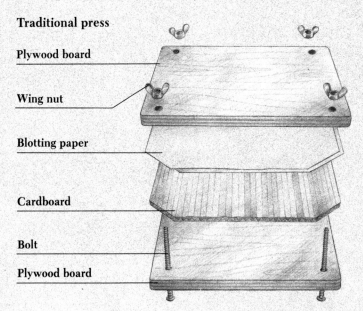

Plywood board

Wing nut

Blotting paper

Cardboard

Bolt

Plywood board

Assembled press

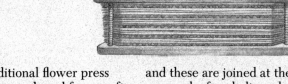

A traditional flower press can be purchased from craft shops or general stores. Alternatively, you could make one at home. Two squares of heavy-gauge plywood form the top and bottom boards of the press, and these are joined at the corners by four bolts and wing nuts. Seven or eight layers of cardboard and blotting paper sheets will fit between the boards, so many flowers and leaves can be pressed at once.

Using a simple press

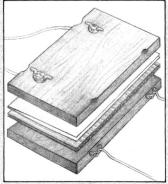

Two heavy mahogany boards are clamped with two nylon threads secured to two cleats fixed to the top board.

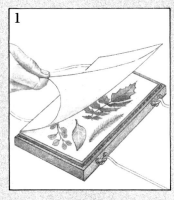

1 Cover the base board with cardboard and place a folded piece of blotting paper on top. Insert the plant material.

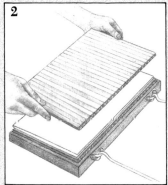

2 Cover the blotting paper with cardboard and continue layering until all your plant material is inserted.

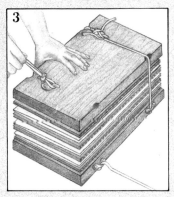

3 Loop the end of each thread around its cleat, then pull the other ends tight and hitch them on the cleats.

Flowers with bulky stamens

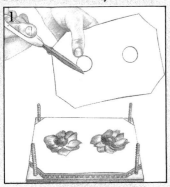

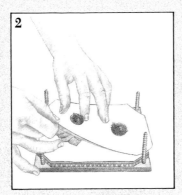

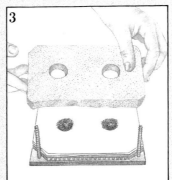

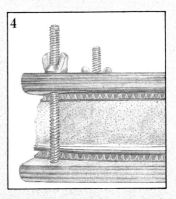

1 For flowers with bulky centres cut holes in the blotting paper the same size as the flower centres.

2 Place the blotting paper over the flowers so that only the stamens peep through the holes.

3 Cut a slice of foam as deep as the stamens, make holes in it as before, and place it on the paper.

4 Cover the foam with a piece of cardboard and continue to load the press until it is filled.

Pressing under the carpet

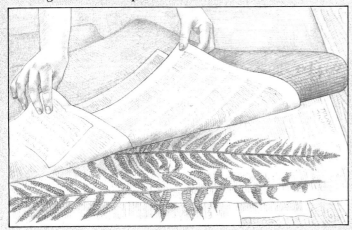

Larger pieces of foliage such as oak, maple, beech and ferns, can be pressed under the carpet (left). Place the foliage between sheets of newspaper on the floor area (not a general thoroughfare). Smaller flower-heads such as pansies and roses, and specimen leaves, can be dried between pieces of blotting or newspaper in a book (right). Weight the top of the book for best results.

Pressing in a book

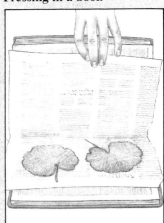

The dried result

This selection of pansies, stachys, hosta, hellebore, hydrangea, alchemilla, dryopteris, senecio and mahonia have all been dried by pressing.

REPAIRS & ALTERATIONS

Much dried plant material is fragile and therefore easily broken. However, the damage caused can often be successfully repaired. If a flower-head comes away from its stem, providing there is still a small amount of stem attached to the flower-head, a new stem can easily be created. Bind wire, another stem or cane to the side of the short, natural stem and cover the whole with gutta-percha tape to conceal the false stem. Most grasses, poppy and onion seedheads, larkspur, achillea, physalis, carthamus and dahlias all have hollow stems. These are simple to repair if they break in two, by inserting one end of a piece of stub wire into the flower-head stem and the other end into the broken piece of stem. Push the bottom piece of stem towards the top piece until they meet, making an almost invisible join, as shown right. Hollow stems can be lengthened in a similar way, if necessary. Insert a stub wire of the required length into the end of the stem and cover with gutta-percha tape to conceal the wire (see also p.65).

Alterations

The shape or colour of some plant material can be changed to stunning effect in your arrangements. The naturally pinky-green outer casings of honesty seed pods can be removed to reveal the mother-of-pearl-like centre filaments. Natural and altered pods look beautiful when set side-by-side in an arrangement. Instead of removing the outer casing of a sweet corn seedhead, you might like to leave it intact as it sometimes develops a beautiful pinky-beige sheen. The seedheads of Chinese lanterns can be split to look like the petals of an open flower. This alteration is best carried out when the lantern is not too dry, or it will split horizontally as the "petals" are pulled back.

Rejoining stems

 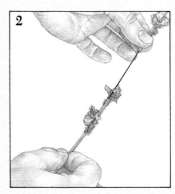

1 To repair a break in a hollow-stemmed plant, insert a piece of stub wire at least 5 cm (2 in) into the top piece of stem, leaving at least 5 cm (2 in) of wire exposed.

2 Push the lower piece of stem over the exposed length of stub wire until the two pieces of stem meet to form a neat join, covering the wire completely.

Lengthening stems

 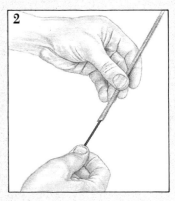

1 To lengthen a hollow stem, take a piece of stub wire long enough to extend the stem to the length required, and of a gauge to fit tightly inside the stem.

2 Insert the stub wire 5–7.5 cm (2–3 in) inside the stem. Cover the whole stem and stub wire with gutta-percha tape so that the extension is concealed.

Wiring a heavy head

 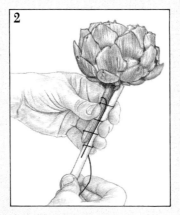  

1 To lengthen a heavy-headed flower stem, such as a globe artichoke, place a piece of cane against it.

2 Hold a medium-gauge stub wire against the cane, bend it and use the long end to bind the two stems.

3 Cover the wire and stems with gutta-percha tape by winding it down from the top at an angle.

4 The top of the false stem will probably be visible just below the flower-head. Cut it off at an angle.

Changing colour (below)
Rub away the two outer casings of honesty when the pinky-green seedheads are about to drop in autumn, to expose the striking silver centre filaments that resemble mother-of-pearl.

Skeletonizing leaves (below)
Skeletonized leaves can be found on the forest floor but they are likely to be partly damaged. To skeletonize strong plant material, such as ivy, laurel, camellia and magnolia leaves yourself, boil them in a solution of 115 g (4 oz) soda crystals and 1 l (2 pt) water for about an hour. Then gently rub away the fleshy green surfaces of the leaves with a soft toothbrush to expose their veined structures.

Changing shape

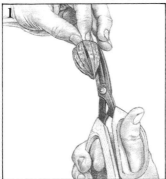

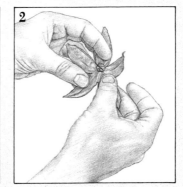

1 To open the orange lanterns of physalis, make four cuts along the veins from the top of the lantern to the base of the head.

2 Gently pull down the four segments created by cutting, to form the open "petals" of an unusual "flower".

Modifications
Chinese lanterns are converted into petalled flowers (right) and a spray of silvery honesty has its outer casings removed (below).

Dried plant material does not have to be used in arrangements straight away, it can be stored for several months without deteriorating. Hang-drying bunches can be decorative in their own right if you have plenty of available space (see pp.122–3). The most space-efficient way of storing dried plant material is to take loose bunches, or separate larger dried flowers, and pack them into cardboard boxes in layers, supporting the flower-heads, if necessary, with crumpled newspaper or tissue paper. The size of the cardboard boxes you use depends entirely on how much material you have to store. The boxes in which flower shops receive fresh flowers are ideal for storing dried flowers and it is a good idea to ask your local flower shop to let you have some, as the boxes are usually thrown away as soon as the fresh flowers have been unpacked.

Packing boxes

There are various methods of packing boxes with dried flowers, shown on this and the following two pages. Which you choose depends on the size and nature of the bunches you intend storing. The standard method for bunches of flowers is shown at the bottom of the page opposite, where you pack the bunches in overlapping ranks. If the bunches you want to store have long stems and lie flat, then you can arrange them flat in layers as shown below right. If the bunches are of plants with delicate flower-heads, particularly of roses, wrap the bunches individually before storing, as shown at the top of page 182.

Pack large-headed plant material, such as delphiniums, paeonies and thistles, singly, securing the stems to the base of the cardboard box with short pieces of masking tape and supporting the heads on crumpled pieces of newspaper or tissue paper. Very delicate flower- and seedheads can be wrapped individually and stored hanging singly or standing in an empty container.

Plant material that has been preserved in glycerine can be stored in a box in the same way as dried material but preserved material must not be mixed with dry material as the moisture it contains will cause dehydrated material placed next to it to rot. Remember that at any stage of the drying and storing process, your work can be ruined by allowing the material to lie in a damp atmosphere. It is a good idea to store boxes of dried material in a cupboard already used for drying plant material. Unpacked dried material could also sit and hang alongside drying material without any ill effects. Make sure the cupboard is well ventilated or, alternatively, install a small electric fan to keep the air circulating.

Choosing healthy specimens

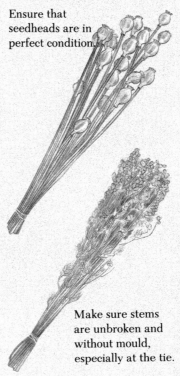

Ensure that seedheads are in perfect condition.

Check bunches for broken or damaged flower- or seedheads.

Make sure stems are unbroken and without mould, especially at the tie.

Split bulrush heads

When buying dried material make sure that there are no signs of rotting or mould, especially at the point of the tie. Check for broken stems and damaged flower- or seedheads. If bulrush heads have not been treated with fixative they may show signs of splitting.

Packing flat material

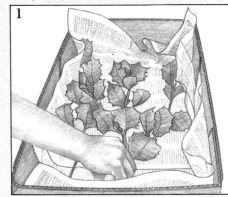

1

2

1 To pack flat dried plant material, place a layer of lightly ruffled newspaper in the bottom of the box. Place the material in rows across the box, until the base of the box is completely covered.

2 Add another layer of crumpled newspaper and cover with plant material as before. Continue layering until the material is about 2.5 cm (1 in) from the top of the box. Cover with newspaper and the lid.

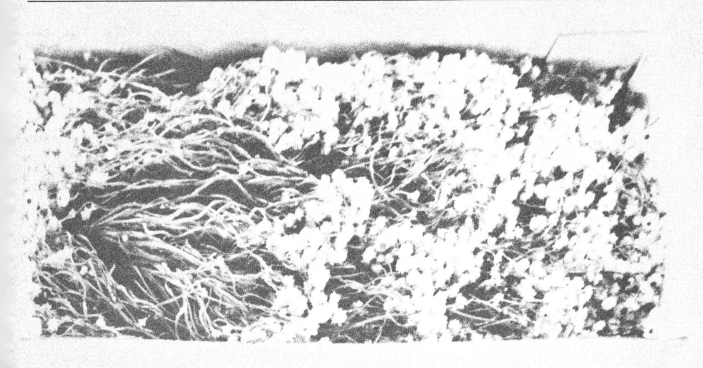

Packing dried flower bunches

1 To pack dried flowers, lay a row of bunches at one end of a box with their heads nearly touching the top edge. Cover the ends of the stems with a strip of tissue paper.

2 Lay the flower-heads of the next row of bunches carefully on the tissue paper. The more delicate the flower-heads being packed, the more tissue paper will be required.

3 Fill three-quarters of the box and then begin packing from the other end. If necessary, thread string through holes in the box to hold the bunches.

Storing in a cupboard

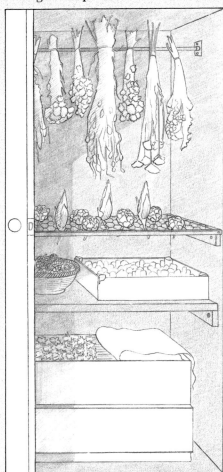

You might like to fit out a cupboard for storing dried flowers and plants. Bunches of drying or dried material can be hung from a pole suspended from the top of the cupboard (see p.172). Heavy-headed material can be supported in a rack of chicken-wire fixed to battens on either side of the cupboard (see p.171). A basket of cones or a box of moss might stand on a shelf, and boxes of dried plant material could be stacked at the bottom of the cupboard.

Wrapping delicate bunches

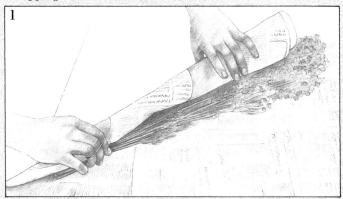

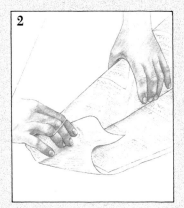

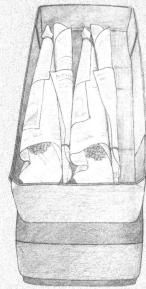

1   When storing bunches of delicate-headed flowers, such as roses, wrap each bunch in newspaper before packing them in a box. Roll a sheet of newspaper loosely around the bunch to form a cone shape. Fold the edge in once to make the cone of flowers more secure.

2   Tuck in the narrow end of the cone as you roll and, when you have wrapped the bunch, secure it with sticky tape or a small elastic band.

Pack the bunches in a box top to tail.

Wrapping individual hydrangeas

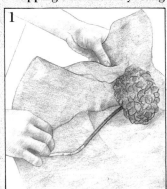

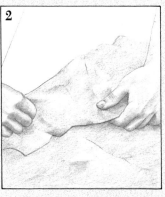

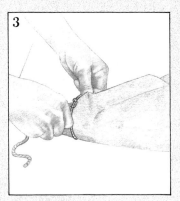

1   Hydrangea heads are fragile and should be individually wrapped before storing. Place each head on a large sheet of tissue paper.

2   Form a loose cone around the flower, taking care not to crush the head. Secure the tissue paper with a small piece of adhesive tape.

3   Take a long piece of string or raffia and tie the cone about 2.5 cm (1 in) from the bottom. Form a hanging loop with the remainder.

Hang individually wrapped flowers to dry.

Wrapping an onion seedhead

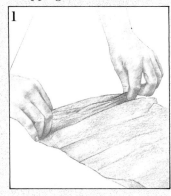

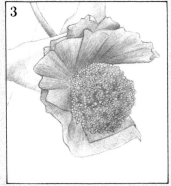

1   To protect a delicate seedhead on a strong stem, pleat a strip of tissue paper 18–20 cm (7–8 in) wide and 60 cm (2 ft) long.

2   Hold the pleated tissue 5 cm (2 in) below the seedhead and fan out the pleats carefully to form a ruff around the head.

3   Secure the tissue paper wrapping by making a string or raffia tie just below the protective paper ruff at the top of the stem.

Store standing upright in an empty container.

SELECTION GUIDE

An enormous range of plant material can be dried and used in arrangements. The following chart makes the task of choosing material that much easier, by providing you with all the essential information at a glance. The common and latin name of each plant is listed, together with the page on which it is illustrated. The overall colour and approximate stem length is given, together with the best time to pick the plant and the best parts to use. The most appropriate drying method is highlighted and the degree of difficulty involved in drying each plant is indicated by the amount of bullets shown. • Easy •• Intermediate ❖ Difficult

Silver	White	Cream	Purple	Blue	Green	Brown	Yellow	Orange	Pink	Red	Specimen length in cm	Colour / Name	Spring	Summer	Autumn	Winter	Flower-head	Spray	Leaf	Seedhead	Air drying	Glycerine	Dessicant	Pressing
						•					30–60	*Acacia* sp. Mimosa/Wattle 30	•				•	•			•			
•											30–60	*Acacia* sp. Mimosa/Wattle 54	•				•	•			•			
	•										60–90	*Acanthus spinosus* Bear's breeches 58			•		•				•			
							•				60	*Achillea filipendulina* 'Coronation Gold' Deep yellow yarrow 29		•			•				•			
									•		60	*Achillea millefolium* Yarrow 25	•				•				•			
							•				60–90	*Achillea* sp. Golden yarrow 31	•				•				•			
							•				60	*Achillea* sp. Light golden yarrow 31	•				•				•			
							•				50	*Achillea* sp. Small-headed yarrow 33	•				•				•			
			•								60–90	*Aconitum napellus* Monkshood 50	•				•				••			
	•										45	*Agonis juniperina* Willow-myrtle 57		•					•		•			
	•										50	*Agonis* sp. White ti-tree		•				•			•			
								•			30	*Aira* sp. Hair-grass 20		•						•	•			
								•			30	*Aira* sp. Hair-grass 21		•						•	•			
					•		•				30	*Alchemilla mollis* Lady's mantle 30	•				•		•		•			•
						•					60–90	*Allium aflatunense* Ornamental onion 44		•						•	•			
								•			45	*Allium* sp. Onion 20		•						•	•			
				•							60–90	*Allium* sp. Onion 59		•						•	•			
					•						45	*Alyssum* sp. Alyssum 38	•						•		•			
					•						30–45	*Amaranthus caudatus* 'Viridis' Love-lies-bleeding 39	•						•		•			
			•								30–45	*Amaranthus* sp. Love-lies-bleeding 50, 51	•							•	•			
	•										45	*Ammobium* sp. Sandflower/Winged everlasting 57	•				•				•			
					•						60	*Anethum graveolens* Dill 36		•			•				••			
										•	60–90	*Anigozanthos rufus* Red kangaroo paw 25		•			•				•			
								•			60–90	*Anigozanthos* sp. Yellow kangaroo paw 29		•			•				•			
					•						60–90	*Anigozanthos* sp. Kangaroo paw 60		•			•				•			
	•										15–30	*Anthemis nobilis* Common chamomile 55	•				•				•			
	•										30	*Aphyllanthes* sp. Grass daisy 59	•				•				•			
							•				25	*Arctosis* sp. African daisy 30	•				•				•			
						•					90–120	*Artemisia vulgaris* Mugwort 42	•						•		•			
					•						150–240	*Arundinaria* sp. Bamboo 37	•	•					•	•	•			
					•						150–180	*Arundinaria* sp. Bamboo 38	•	•					•	•	•			
					•						120–150	*Arundinaria* sp. Bamboo 41	•	•					•	•	•			
			•								60	*Astilbe davidii* Astilbe 50, 51	•				•				•			
								•			60	*Banksia attenuata* Australian honeysuckle 31	•				•				•			
								•			60	*Banksia baxteri* Australian honeysuckle 30	•				•				•			
									•		60	*Banksia menziesii* Australian honeysuckle 21	•				•				•			
									•		90	*Banksia occidentalis* Australian honeysuckle 21	•				•		•		•			
	•										90	*Banksia prionotes* Australian honeysuckle 60	•				•				•			
					•						90	*Banksia* sp. Banksia 37	•						•		•			
						•					60 +	*Betula pendula* Silver birch 43			•			•			•			
					•						45	*Briza maxima* Big or large quaking grass 36, 37		•						•	•			
								•			30–45	*Briza media* Common quaking grass 21		•						•	•			
					•						30	*Briza minima* Lesser or small quaking grass 36		•						•	•			
								•			45	*Bromus* sp. Brome grass 20		•						•	•			
	•				•						60	*Bupleurum* sp. Bupleurum 55		•			•		•		•			
		•									45	*Cacalia* sp. Tassel flower 59	•				•				•			
						•					45	*Calamus* sp. Rattan palm/Wait-awhile vine 42	•				•				•			
								•			30	*Calendula officinalis* Pot marigold 33	•				•						••	•
										•	60	*Callistemon beaufortia sparsa* Red bottlebrush 23	•				•				•			
					•						60–90	*Callistemon citrinus* Crimson bottlebrush 41	•						•	•	•			
					•						45	*Calytrix* sp. Fringe myrtle 38	•						•		•			

183

Silver	White	Cream	Purple	Blue	Green	Brown	Yellow	Orange	Pink	Red	Specimen length in cm	Name	Spring	Summer	Autumn	Winter	Flower-head	Spray	Leaf	Seedhead	Air drying	Glycerine	Dessicant	Pressing
					●						30	*Capsella* sp. Cress 38	●							●	●			
						●					60–75	*Carex* sp. Sedge 45		●						●	●			
●											30	*Carlina acaulis* 'Caulescens' Stemless thistle 58		●			●				●			
								●			60–90	*Carthamus tinctorius* Safflower/Dyer's saffron 33	●				●				●			
										●	25	*Celastrus* sp. Celastrus 24		●						●	●●			
								●	●	●	30	*Celosia argentea cristata* Celosia cockscomb 25	●				●				●			
			●	●							30	*Centaurea cyanus* Cornflower 50, 51	●				●				●●			
●											45	*Cephalipterum drummondii* Silver-flowered everlastings 55	●				●				●			
		●									45	*Chenopodium* sp. Chenopodium 39	●							●	●			
	●										120–150	*Chenopodium* sp. Chenopodium 59	●						●		●			
	●	●									30+	*Choisya ternata* Mexican orange 41		●			●		●			●		●
							●				60	*Chrysanthemum* sp. Tansy 30		●			●				●			
							●				60	*Chrysanthemum* sp. Chrysanthemum 32		●			●				●			
							●				60	*Chrysanthemum vulgare* Tansy 32		●			●				●			
●											5	*Cladonia* sp. Lichen 60		●	●				●		●			
		●									25	*Clematis* sp. Clematis seedhead 60		●						●	●			
	●										15	*Clematis vitalba* Old man's beard/Travellers' joy/Wild clematis 60		●					●		●			
	●			●					●		60–90	*Consolida* sp. Larkspur 22	●				●				●			
	●										150–270	*Cortaderia selloana* Pampas grass 54		●						●	●			
	●										150–270	*Cortaderia selloana* Pampas grass 57		●						●	●●			
	●										150–270	*Cortaderia selloana* Pampas grass 59		●						●	●●			
							●				30	*Craspedia globosa* Craspedia 28	●				●				●			
						●					120–150	*Cynara scolymus* Globe artichoke 44		●			●				●			
									●		60	*Cynara* sp. Pink cardoon 20		●			●				●			
						●					60	*Cyperus papyrus* Egyptian paper rush/Papyrus 45	●							●	●			
	●						●	●	●		30–60	*Dahlia* sp. Pom-pom dahlia 25	●				●				●●		●●	
	●			●					●		60–90	*Delphinium consolida* Larkspur 48	●				●				●●		●●	
				●							90	*Delphinium elatum* Perennial delphinium 50	●	●			●				●●		●●	
				●							60	*Delphinium* sp. Small-flowered delphinium 51	●						●		●			
		●									90	*Delphinium* sp. Cream delphinium 56	●	●			●				●●		●●	
	●										90	*Delphinium* sp. White delphinium 57	●	●			●				●●		●●	
	●										90	*Dianthus* sp. Pink fruits 58	●							●				
							●				60	*Dryandra formosa* Golden dryandra	●				●				●			
							●				60	*Dryandra polycephala* Golden (prickly) dryandra	●						●		●			
							●				30–60	*Dryandra quercifolia* Dryandra 31	●				●				●			
					●						60	*Dryandra* sp. Dryandra 40	●				●				●			
					●						60	*Dryopteris filix-mas* Male fern 38	●						●		●			
				●							60	*Echinops ritro* Miniature globe thistle 48		●			●				●●			
				●							60–90	*Echinops ritro* Globe thistle 48, 49	●				●				●●			
									●		30–60	*Erica cinerea* Bell heather 24		●			●				●			
				●							60	*Eryngium* sp. Eryngium 49		●			●				●			
●											60	*Eucalyptus cinerea* Silver-dollar gum 60		●					●			●		
					●	●					90	*Eucalyptus ficifolia* Bloodwood (large gumnuts)		●	●					●	●			
●											30–60	*Eucalyptus globulus* Tasmanian blue gum 54		●					●		●	●		
					●	●					90	*Eucalyptus gummifera* Sydney bloodwood (gumnuts)		●	●					●	●			
					●						60–90	*Eucalyptus niphophila* Snow gum 40		●					●	●	●			
						●					60	*Eucalyptus* sp. Bronze-leaved eucalpytus 25		●					●		●			
●											30–60	*Eucalyptus tetragona* White mallee eucalyptus 60		●					●		●			
					●						60–90	*Fagus sylvatica* Beech 38	●					●	●		●			●
			●								60–90	*Fagus sylvatica* 'Cuprea' Copper beech 24	●					●	●		●			●
									●		30–60	*Festuca* sp. Pink fescue grass 20		●						●	●			
									●		30–60	*Festuca* sp. Pale pink fescue grass 21		●						●	●			
							●				30–60	*Festuca* sp. Fescue grass 45		●						●	●			
	●								●		45	*Gomphrena globosa* Globe amaranth 23	●				●				●●			
	●										60–90	*Gossypium herbaceum* Cotton 57	●							●	●			
		●									60+	*Grevillea* sp. Australian spider bush 39	●						●		●			
					●						5	*Grimmia pulvinata* Grimmia moss/Bun moss 39			●		●				●			
	●										45	*Gypsophila* sp. Baby's breath 56		●			●				●			
		●									30+	*Hakea cucullata* Hakea 38		●					●		●			
		●	●								60–90	*Hakea* sp. Hakea 41		●					●		●			
		●									30	*Hedera helix* Ivy 38	●	●			●					●●		●●

Silver	White	Cream	Purple	Blue	Green	Brown	Yellow	Orange	Pink	Red	Specimen length in cm	Name	Spring	Summer	Autumn	Winter	Flower-head	Spray	Leaf	Seedhead	Air drying	Glycerine	Dessicant	Pressing
							•				25	*Helichrysum angustifolium* Curry plant/Stinking everlasting 28	•				•				•			
								•			45	*Helichrysum bracteatum* Peach everlasting/Strawflower 22	•				•				•			
										•	45	*Helichrysum bracteatum* Rich red everlasting/Strawflower 24	•				•				•			
										•	45	*Helichrysum bracteatum* Deep red everlasting/Strawflower 25	•				•				•			
		•									45	*Helichrysum bracteatum* Strawflower 58	•				•				•			
•											60	*Helichrysum cordatum* Seacrest 56	•					•			•			
							•				30	*Helichrysum italicum* Cluster-flowered everlasting/Strawflower 28	•				•				•			
							•				45	*Helichrysum* sp. Pale yellow everlasting/Strawflower 28	•				•				•			
							•				45	*Helichrysum* sp. Golden everlasting/Strawflower 29	•				•				•			
							•				25	*Helichrysum* sp. Silver-leaved everlasting/Strawflower 29	•				•				•			
	•										15	*Helichrysum* sp. Miniature cluster-flowered everlasting 54, 55	•				•				•			
•											45	*Helichrysum* sp. Everlasting silver foliage 55	•						•		•			
•											25	*Helichrysum* sp. Silver everlasting/Strawflower 56	•				•				•			
									•		45	*Helipterum manglesii* Swan River everlasting 22	•				•				•			
	•										45	*Helipterum manglesii* Sunray 56	•				•				•			
									•		45	*Helipterum roseum* Sunray 22	•				•				•			
									•		45	*Helipterum* sp. Sunray 23	•				•				•			
							•				45	*Helipterum* sp. Sunray 29	•				•				•	•		
	•										45	*Helipterum* sp. Large-flowered sunray 56	•				•				•			
	•										15	*Helipterum* sp. Miniature sunray 57	•				•				•			
			•								25	*Helipterum* sp. Cluster-flowered sunray 59	•				•				•			
	•										90 +	*Heracleum sphondylium* Hogweed 59		•						•	•			
						•					45	*Hordeum* sp. Black-eared barley 42		•						•	•			
					•						45	*Hordeum vulgare* Six-rowed barley 37		•						•	•			
	•				•						45	*Hosta* sp. Plantain lily (fruit) 58		•					•	•	•			•
					•						45	*Humulus lupulus* Hop 44		•					•	•	•	•		
					•						30–60	*Hydrangea macrophylla* Mop-headed hydrangea 37		•			•				•	•		
					•						30–60	*Hydrangea macrophylla* Mop-headed hydrangea 40		•			•				•	•		
				•							30–60	*Hydrangea macrophylla* Blue-tinged hydrangea florets 49		•			•				•	•		
			•								30–60	*Hydrangea macrophylla* Mop-headed hydrangea 58		•			•				•	•		
			•								30–60	*Hydrangea macrophylla* 'Generale Vicomtesse de Vibraye' Mop-headed hydrangea 48		•			•				•	•		
									•		30–60	*Hydrangea macrophylla* Mop-headed hydrangea 21		•			•				•	•		
					•						30–60	*Hydrangea paniculata* Panicled hydrangea 37		•			•				•	•		
	•										30	*Ixodia achilleoides* South Australian daisy 30	•	•			•				•			
	•										30	*Ixodia* sp. South Australian daisy 57	•				•				•			
					•						60	*Juncus* sp. Rush 40		•					•		•			
					•						45	*Kingia australis* Dgingarra leaf 56	•						•		•			
	•										30	*Lachnostachys* sp. Lachnostachys 56	•				•				•			
		•									45	*Lapsana* sp. Nipplewort 58		•						•	•			
						•					15	*Larix* sp. Larch cone 43		•						•	•			
			•								30–45	*Lavandula spica* Lavender 48	•				•				•	•		
						•					30	*Lecythis usitata* Paradise nut/Sapucia nut 42		•						•	•			
								•			30	*Leptospermum* sp. Silver strawberry 23	•				•				•			
						•					30–60	*Leucodendron rubrum* Tolbos/Top-brush 42	•				•				•			
									•		30	*Leucodendron* sp. Leucodendron 25	•				•				•			
					•						30	*Leucodendron* sp. Leucodendron 40	•						•		•			
					•	•					45	*Leucodendron* sp. Leucodendron 45	•						•		•			
						•					30–60	*Leucodendron stelligenum* Leucodendron 41	•						•		•			
		•									30–40	*Liatris* sp. Button snakeroot/Blazing star/Kansas gayfeather 60	•				•				•			

Silver	White	Cream	Purple	Blue	Green	Brown	Yellow	Orange	Pink	Red	Colour — Specimen length in cm	Plant	Spring	Summer	Autumn	Winter	Flower-head	Spray	Leaf	Seedhead	Air drying	Glycerine	Dessicant	Pressing
									●		30–40	*Liatris spicata* Button snakeroot/Blazing star/Kansas gayfeather 24		●			●				●			
			●								45	*Limonium sinuatum* Mauve statice 50	●				●				●			
			●								45	*Limonium sinuatum* Purple statice 51	●				●				●			
			●								45	*Limonium sinuatum* Pink-purple statice 51	●				●				●			
									●		45	*Limonium* sp. Salmon-pink statice 23	●				●				●			
							●				45	*Limonium* sp. Golden-flowered statice 30	●				●				●			
								●			45	*Limonium* sp. Deep salmon-pink statice 32	●				●				●			
				●							30–45	*Limonium* sp. Large-flowered sea lavender 48	●				●				●			
				●							30	*Limonium* sp. Sea lavender 49	●				●				●			
	●										60	*Limonium* sp. Sea lavender 54	●				●				●			
	●										30	*Limonium* sp. Sea lavender 57	●				●				●			
		●									45	*Limonium* sp. Cream statice 57	●				●				●			
	●										45	*Limonium* sp. Sea lavender 60	●				●				●			
									●		45–60	*Limonium suworowii* Russian statice/Rat's tail statice 24	●				●				●			
									●		45–60	*Lunaria rediviva* Honesty 20		●						●	●			
●											45–60	*Lunaria rediviva* Honesty (prepared) 60		●						●	●			
			●								90+	*Macrozamina communis* Burrawongs	●	●	●	●			●				●	
●											45	*Melaleuca* sp. Melaleuca 55	●							●	●			
					●						45–60	*Milium* sp. Millet 44			●					●	●			
					●						1–5	*Mnium* sp. Moss 38	●						●		●			
		●									30–60	*Moluccella laevis* Bells of Ireland/Shell flower 58	●					●			●	●	●	●
						●					25	*Nelumbo lucifera* Lotus flower (fruits) 43			●					●	●			
				●							45	*Nigella damascena* Love-in-a-mist 39	●							●	●			
				●							45	*Nigella damascena* Love-in-a-mist 44	●							●	●			
●											60	*Olearia* sp. Daisy bush 55	●							●	●			
									●		45	*Paeonia lactiflora* Paeony 21	●				●				●		●	
	●										45	*Papaver rhoeas* Field poppy (fruit) 59	●							●	●		●	
									●		60	*Pennisetum* sp. Pennisetum 21		●						●	●			
									●		30	*Phaenocoma prolifera* Phaenocoma shrub 23	●				●				●			
					●						45	*Phalaris arundinacea* Reed canary grass 37	●							●	●			
					●						45	*Phleum pratense* Timothy 37	●							●	●			
●							●				30–45	*Phlomis fruticosa* Jerusalem sage 30	●				●		●	●	●			
					●						45	*Phragmites australis* Reed 40, 41, 43	●	●						●	●			
								●			60	*Physalis alkekengi franchetti* Chinese lantern/Bladder cherry 32		●						●	●			
					●						60	*Physocarpus* sp. Physocarpus 45	●							●	●			
					●						10	*Pinus ayacahuite* Mexican white pine cone 43		●						●	●			
					●						10	*Pinus* sp. Pine cone 42		●						●	●			
				●	●						60	*Pinus sylvestris* Scots pine 40		●					●		●			
					●						5	*Pinus sylvestris* Scots pine cone 43		●						●	●			
	●										45	*Pithocarpa corymbulosa* Miniature everlasting 55	●				●				●			
									●		30	*Protea compacta* Protea/Cape honey flower 20	●				●				●			
●											30+	*Protea* sp. Protea/Cape honey flower 60	●				●				●			
					●						30+	*Quercus palustris* Pin oak 36	●						●			●		
						●					30+	*Quercus palustris* Pin oak 43	●						●					●
							●				25	*Ranunculus* sp. Buttercup 32	●				●				●			
					●						90+	*Reseda lutea* Wild mignonette 38		●			●				●			
										●	25	*Rosa* cv. Vermillion floribunda rose 22	●				●						●	
								●			25	*Rosa* cv. Terracotta miniature rose 23	●				●						●	
							●				25+	*Rosa* cv. Orange-yellow hybrid tea rose 33	●				●						●	
								●			25+	*Rosa* 'Gerda' Pink-tinged hybrid tea rose 22	●				●						●	
							●				25+	*Rosa* 'Golden Times' Deep yellow hybrid tea rose 28	●				●						●	
										●	50	*Rosa* 'Ilona' Deep scarlet hybrid tea rose 24	●				●						●	
	●										25+	*Rosa* 'Jack Frost' White-flowering hybrid tea rose 58	●				●						●	
										●	25+	*Rosa* 'Jaguar' Scarlet-tinged hybrid tea rose 25	●				●						●	
								●			25+	*Rosa* 'La Minuette' Bronze-tinged hybrid tea rose 29	●				●						●	
			●								25	*Rosa* 'Lilac Paleander' Lilac-tinged miniature rose 49	●				●						●	
										●	25+	*Rosa* 'Mercedes' Cerise-tinged hybrid tea rose 23	●				●						●	
						●					120+	*Rumex* sp. Dock/Sorrel 33		●					●		●			
		●									90+	*Scirpus* sp. Clubrush 36	●								●			

Silver	White	Cream	Purple	Blue	Green	Brown	Yellow	Orange	Pink	Red	Specimen length in cm	Colour / Name	Spring	Summer	Autumn	Winter	Flower-head	Spray	Leaf	Seedhead	Air drying	Glycerine	Dessicant	Pressing
					●						60–90	*Scirpus* sp. Clubrush 41		●						●	●			
				●							15	*Selaginella* sp. Clubmoss 39	●						●		●	●	● ●	
●											40	*Senecio greyi* Senecio 54	●						●				●	
●											45	*Serruria* sp. Silky serruria 56	●						●		●			
				●							45	*Setaria verticillata* Rough bristle grass 37	●						●		●			
									●		30	*Silene* sp. Campion 22	●				●				●	●		
			●								60 +	*Solidago canadensis* Golden rod 31		●			●				●			
							●				60 +	*Solidago canadensis* 'Lemore' Golden rod 39		●			●				●			
					●						5	*Sphagnum* sp. Sphagnum moss 58	●						●		●			
					●						5	*Sphagnum* sp. Sphagnum moss 59	●						●		●			
●											25 +	*Stachys lanata* Lamb's tongue 54	●				●						●	
●											60	*Stirlingia latifolia* Stirlingia 55	●					●			●			
					●						50 +	*Tilia* sp. Lime 36	●					●						●
						●					90	*Typha angustifolia* Lesser reedmace 42		●						●	● ●			
						●					120	*Typha latifolia* Greater reedmace 42		●						●	● ●			
●											45 +	*Verbascum* sp. Mullein 54	●					●						
		●									45	*Verticordia brownii* Cauliflower morrison	●					●			●			
							●				45	*Verticordia nitens* Golden morrison	●					●			●			
									●		45	*Verticordia* sp. Feather flower 31	●					●			●			
									●		45	*Verticorda* sp. Feather flower 59	●					●			●			
		●									80 +	*Xanthorrhoea* sp. Glasstree spears			●		●							
●											15 +	*Xylomelum angustifolium* Woody pear 58		●						●	● ●			
								●			120	*Zea mays* Sweet corn (fruit) 33		●						●	● ●			

LIST OF SUPPLIERS

Dried flowers can be obtained from **National Trust Shops**

London has many stockists, including:
Conran Shop
77 Fulham Road SW3
The Flowering Dutchman
153 Ladbroke Grove W10
General Trading Company
144 Sloane Street SW1
Habitat branches
Harrods
Knightsbridge SW1
Heal's
196 Tottenham Court Road W1
Hillier & Hilton
Plants & Flowers
98 Church Road
Barnes SW13
Next branches

The following shops, listed alphabetically by town or city, stock a wide range of dried flowers

Hayes Garden World
Lake Road
Ambleside Cumbria

Cullens Florist
88-92 Henrietta Street
Aston-under-Lyne
Lancashire

The Country Garden
19 Winston Square
Barry
South Glamorgan

Collections
4-5 Green Street
Bath Avon

Flowers and Gardens
Kensington London Road
Bath Avon

Margaret Tregoning
11 Cannon Street
Birmingham

Hilliers Garden Centres
Botley, Liss, Winchester and
Sunningdale

Southern County Giftware
22 Bridal Crescent
Bournemouth Dorset

The Warehouse
North Street
Burnham Market Norfolk

Barkways
245 Cathedral Road
Cardiff

Pine Box
9 Royal Parade
Chislehurst Kent

Mens Gallery
23 Killinchy Street
Comber
Northern Ireland

Scotfresh
30 Galloway Street
Dumfries
Scotland

Edinburgh Flower Shop
33 George Street
Edinburgh
Scotland

Jenners
Princes Street
Edinburgh
Scotland

Redfields Nursery and Garden Centre
Ewshot Lane
Fleet Aldershot
Hampshire

Rodney Kent
20 West Park
Harrogate
North Yorkshire

Blossoms Florist of Henley Ltd
44 Bell Street
Henley-on-Thames
Oxfordshire

Flowers Unlimited
1 Bank Street
Hythe Kent

Bunches
67 Goodmayes Road
Ilford Essex

Floreander
West Street
Lewes East Sussex

Lema Gifts
299 High Road
Loughton
Essex

Tokenhouse
Bridlesmith Gate
Nottingham

Jem-i-ni Ltd
39-40 The Market
Oxford

Frances Watterson
7 Athell Place
Peel
Isle of Man

Baileys
72 High Street
Rochester
Kent

Daisy Chain
58 Street Lane
Roundhay
Leeds

Florabunda
14 Hatfield Road
St Albans
Hertfordshire

Park Plaza Florest
73 Market Place
St Helier
Jersey

Flower Basket
25 Frankwell
Shrewsbury

Arabis
246 Blackfen Road
Sidcup
Kent

Keddies
High Street
Southend
Essex

Mayflower
8 Gold Street
Tiverton
Devon

Whitacott Dried Flowers
Langtree
Torrington
North Devon

Agora Craft Gallery
12 High Street
Wendover
Buckinghamshire

Art of Flowers
91 Clover Hill Road
Windsor
Berkshire

189

Authors' acknowledgments
We wish to thank Andreas Einsiedel and Sally Smallwood for all their creative help; David Lamb, Jane Laing and Jane Warring for all their editing and design work; Sue Newth for her wonderful support, together with Lala Benn and Angela Murphey at Hillier and Hilton, Barnes, London SW13; also, Eileen Bell, Kitty Black, Kathleen Darby, Peter Day, June Henry, Peter Machin, Mr and Mrs Richard Raworth, Sarah Stone, David White, and Josephine White.

Dorling Kindersley would like to thank Osborne and Little, London SW3, for supplying the wallpaper on pp.78–83; Colin Welland for the arrangement on pp.96–7; David Douglas Carpets Ltd, London SW8, for the carpet on pp.125, 131, 143, 144, 147, 151, 154; Eileen Bell for her painting on p.143; Horse Yard Antiques, London N1, for the pine door on pp.147–8; Fired Earth, London W11, for the floor tiles on p.151; Real Flame, London SW6, for the gas fire on p.151; Matthiae's Bakery, Richmond, for the wedding cake on p.154; Culpeper Ltd, London W1, for the sleep pillow, and wardrobe sachets and pot-pourri on pp.164–5; The Flowering Dutchman, London W10, for their help with the list of suppliers on p.187; Machin and Henry Dried Flowers, London SE8; Andreas Einsiedel, Danny and Steve for photographic assistance; Dr John Feltwell for his valuable help with the ingredients section; Joanna Jellinek for help with editing; Moira Mole and Richard Bird for the index; Tessa Richardson-Jones for help with design; Carolyn Ryden for the initial editing work; Patrizio Semproni for his help with paste-up; and Jimmy Tsao and Mr Sakai for their help in the reproduction and printing of the book.

Illustrators
David Ashby: pp.174–5, 178–9
Tim Foster: pp.170–3, 176–7, 182

Photographic credits
All photography by Andreas Einsiedel, except for: p.11 (top) Alex Starkey, reproduced by kind permission of *Country Life*; p.13 Andrew Lawson; p.14 Andrew Butler; p.15 Eric Crichton; p.16 (bottom) Andrew Lawson; endpapers Andrew Butler.

Typesetting
MS Filmsetting Limited, Frome, Somerset